# EMOTIONS IN A DIGITAL WORLD

AF721985

This book presents an introduction to strategies for qualitative digital social research on emotions in a digital world.

The book emphasizes the connections that exist between emotional ecologies, emotions as texts, and the virtual/mobile/digital world that brings us closer to a hermeneutics of the practices of feeling. In the context of "Society 4.0", the book explores:

- Changes in the organization of daily life and work in virtual, mobile, and digital environments.
- The impact of apps and social networks on sensations, emotions, and sensibilities.
- Necessary changes in social research to employ the power of these apps and networks for social enquiry.

As such, this book shares a set of social inquiry practices developed and applied to capture and understand emotions today. It should be considered as a first step in a long journey of exploring the close connections between sensibilities, emotions, and social research methodology. The book will appeal to students and instructors of emotion studies from across the social sciences, including sociology, psychology, organization studies, ethnography, history, and political science.

**Adrian Scribano** is Director of the Centre for Sociological Research and Studies (CIES estudiosociologicos.org) and Principal Researcher at the National Scientific and Technological Research Council, Argentina. He is also the Director of the *Latin American Journal of Studies on Bodies, Emotions and Society* and the Study Group on Sociology of Emotions and Bodies, in the Gino Germani Research Institute, Faculty of Social Sciences, University of Buenos Aires. He also serves as Coordinator of the 26 Working Group on Bodies and Emotions of the Latin American Association of Sociology (ALAS) and as Vice-President of the Working Group 08 Society and Emotions of the International Sociological Association (ISA).

# EMOTIONS IN A DIGITAL WORLD

## Social Research 4.0

*Adrian Scribano*

Routledge
Taylor & Francis Group
LONDON AND NEW YORK

Designed cover image: Getty Images

First published 2023
by Routledge
4 Park Square, Milton Park, Abingdon, Oxon OX14 4RN

and by Routledge
605 Third Avenue, New York, NY 10158

*Routledge is an imprint of the Taylor & Francis Group, an informa business*

© 2023 Adrian Scribano

The right of Adrian Scribano to be identified as author of this work has been asserted in accordance with sections 77 and 78 of the Copyright, Designs and Patents Act 1988.

All rights reserved. No part of this book may be reprinted or reproduced or utilised in any form or by any electronic, mechanical, or other means, now known or hereafter invented, including photocopying and recording, or in any information storage or retrieval system, without permission in writing from the publishers.

*Trademark notice*: Product or corporate names may be trademarks or registered trademarks, and are used only for identification and explanation without intent to infringe.

*British Library Cataloguing-in-Publication Data*
A catalogue record for this book is available from the British Library

*Library of Congress Cataloging-in-Publication Data*
Names: Scribano, Adrián, author.
Title: Emotions in a digital world: social research 4.0 / Adrian Scribano.
Description: Abingdon, Oxon; New York, NY: Routledge, 2023. |
Includes bibliographical references and index.
Identifiers: LCCN 2022041178 (print) | LCCN 2022041179 (ebook) |
ISBN 9781032334745 (hbk) | ISBN 9781032334554 (pbk) |
ISBN 9781003319771 (ebk)
Subjects: LCSH: Organizational change–Psychological aspects. |
Emotions–Social aspects.
Classification: LCC HD58.8.S43 2023 (print) |
LCC HD58.8 (ebook) | DDC 658.4/06–dc23/eng/20221011
LC record available at https://lccn.loc.gov/2022041178
LC ebook record available at https://lccn.loc.gov/2022041179

ISBN: 978-1-032-33474-5 (hbk)
ISBN: 978-1-032-33455-4 (pbk)
ISBN: 978-1-003-31977-1 (ebk)

DOI: 10.4324/9781003319771

Typeset in Bembo
by Deanta Global Publishing Services, Chennai, India

To Maia Pia.

# CONTENTS

# ILLUSTRATIONS

## Figures



## Table

# ACKNOWLEDGEMENTS

I want to thank Emily Briggs, Mary Holmes, and Julie Brownlie for believing in this project. I also want to thank Lakshita Joshi for the editorial assistance. Finally, this book would not be the same without the invaluable assistance and the enormous contribution of Florencia Chahbenderian.

# INTRODUCTION

## Emotions: Social Research 4.0

In the 1960s, Marshall McLuhan (1964) argued that new technologies had made modifications in our central nervous system possible, since they operated as extensions of our senses.

Instagram, WhatsApp, TikTok, Facebook, and Zoom, among many other applications, have been incorporated into the daily lives of billions of people on a planet, that thanks to the existence of the virtual/mobile/digital world, has become smaller every day.

The social sciences since their inception have modified their strategies of inquiry in line with modifications produced in social structuration processes (*sensu* Giddens).

This book offers an introduction to some strategies of qualitative digital social research on emotions, allowing us to reconstruct their basic components and become familiar with their applications in various topics of contemporary inquiry.

This introduction aims to provide an overview of the motivations of and possible objections to digital connections, as well as an overview of the contents of the book. It aims to introduce the reader to the perspective offered to connect Society 4.0, social research, and emotions.

### I.1 Digital Research

It is possible, necessary, and urgent to study emotions in and through the virtual/mobile/digital world. There are digital ways to elaborate, capture, and understand emotions, and the social sciences have a set of "practices of inquiry" to build knowledge about these processes.

DOI: 10.4324/9781003319771-1

Among many others, there are a set of strategies and quantitative tools for analyzing emotions called sentiment analysis, as Zhang and colleagues argue: "According to the current research methods, there are three main aspects for sentiment analysis including sentiment computing based on semantic dictionary, sentiment classification based on machine learning and other methods" (Zhang et al., 2018, p. 396).

In the context pointed out, sentiment analysis has been used for several years (Gratch et al., 2015) in different fields of social inquiry:

> Sentiment is a long-term disposition evoked when a person encounters a specific topic, person, or entity. Understanding people's position, attitude or opinion towards a certain entity has many applications. For example, companies are interested in understanding how their products or their brand is perceived among their customers. Political parties are interested in opinion polling to gauge voting intentions. Automatic sentiment analysis is the computational understanding of one's position, attitude or opinion towards an entity, person or topic (...). With the advent of the World Wide Web and shortly after, the social web, individuals are enabled to broadly express their opinions through these media (Soleymani et al., 2017, p. 3).
>
> *(p. 891)*

In a diverse line, the book that is introduced here is part of the transformations of qualitative digital social research on emotions in the framework of social changes and the modifications in the methodological strategies that these transformations require.

We are in a time of change; the social sciences and their research strategies are changing as Salganik argues in his book *Bit By Bit. Social Research in the Digital Age*:

> Just as the principles of photography inform those of cinematography, the principles of social research that have been developed over the past 100 years will inform the social research taking place over the next 100 years. But the change also means that we should not just keep doing the same thing. Rather, we must combine the approaches of the past with the capabilities of the present and future.
>
> *(Salganik, 2018, p. 5)*

Modifications in procedures are long-lasting mutations that take what is already known and transform/adapt/reinvent it into the new. The methodology of digital social research is nourished and revitalizes the pre-existing, and improves and creates new/old ways of knowing. In this direction, Marres makes the following point:

> To make sense of this encounter, Richard Rogers (2009) has elaborated a helpful distinction, namely that between the development of "natively

> digital" methods and the "digitization" of methods. Advocates of the former project argue that digital technologies make possible, or even necessitate, the development of "intrinsically new" methods, which take advantage of distinctive features of digital infrastructures, devices and practices (Rogers, 2013; see also Lee et al., 2008). Adherents of the latter approach, by contrast, stress continuity in methodology development across different media and technological settings. They stress the similarities between today's digital data and techniques and their "pre-digital" equivalents and conclude that our main challenge is the implementation of existing methods, such as content analysis or survey research, in digital settings (Herring, 2009; Savage, 2010). The digital then presents social researchers with a basic methodological choice: in conducting digital research, do we seek to translate established methods like ethnography or content analysis into digital forms, or do we seek to develop more experimental, "new" methods that seek to take advantage of the inherent features of digital technologies and practices?
>
> *(Marres, 2017, p. 109)*

This book implies, at the same time, an epistemology and a theory about emotions in the digital age, which generate and give foundation to the methodological strategies explored here. The book presents a set of inquiry practices developed and applied to capture and understand emotions today. The central proposal of the book is to share with readers digital social research strategies that have been applied in what currently constitutes the real-digital *continuum.*

## I.2 Society and Revolution 4.0

Numerous changes in the social structuration processes on a planetary scale occurred in the first 20 years of this century as some consequences of the so-called Revolution 4.0. In this context, three modifications can be pointed out, among others, as processes still in production: a) the change in the forms of organization of daily life and work in virtual/mobile/digital environments, b) the impact that the "applications" and social networks have in sensations, emotions, and sensibilities, and c) the necessary modifications in social research to capture or use the power of said "applications" and networks as part of the processes of social inquiry. The objective of this book is to systematically present, through concrete examples, the basic components for using digital ethnography, Instagram, drones, WhatsApp, and Zoom as instruments of social research.

We live in a virtual/digitally connected world shaped by the technological transformations of the last twenty years. Internet and mobile telephony are two vectors that set the stage for three strong changes in the politics of sensibilities: a) the organization of the day/night unlinked to the experience of the subjects that experience it, b) the modification of the sensations of classification, and c) valuations on world modifications.

In this context, it is possible to understand how the digitalization of the world coexists with the emotionalization of the processes of domination and everyday life. We are facing a social system that is globalized by producing/buying/selling emotions in and through the media, social networks, and the Internet. In this sense, it is possible to understand the emergence of "sensibilities of platform".

Each society has a preponderant way of managing labour, and this constitutes a central axis of the politics of sensibilities. Society 4.0 implies the massification of digital labour. A "sensibilities of platform" emerges in Society 4.0 that is immediate in three senses: a) in the vehicle the action resides in (it is the feeling of always being "online"), b) it is a society that "is during use", "between", "in passing", and c) is pure presentification (here/now). A lot of digital work has the same characteristics, and, in this direction, the political economy of morality consecrates this way of "feeling the world".

Revolution 4.0 is carrier of social practices and modes of interaction where mobile devices play a special role. Mobile communication devices (from cell phones to tablets) have become spaces for production, editing, and a vehicle for storing images. Based on easily accessible and managed programs, the owners of the aforementioned devices have become "image makers", "creators of emotions", "companions of loneliness", and "shopping advisers". The power of programs and devices is more than obvious, and their use in social research is a growing need in the social sciences.

One of the central aspects of the connection between the virtual/mobile/digital world and social science research is to understand that this connection operates in at least three spheres that influence each other.

Firstly, the Internet as a network of knowledge, competencies, and storage of information is at the same time a space for inquiries, an instrument of investigation, and a new modality of knowledge.

Secondly, it is necessary to be able to capture the relationship between information storage, management, and production space, the devices created for such purposes, the modes and tools to produce digitization, and the interactive features of these devices with other instruments and tools of the internet of things and other aspects of Revolution 4.0.

Thirdly, it is necessary to clarify the relationships between standards and instruments of traditional social research, both in their quantitative and qualitative versions, with the new instruments developed by the impact of Revolution 4.0 and the digital perspective of the world.

Within the framework of these three aspects, as three spheres that interact to shape the context of digital social research today, this book is proposed as a beginning, as a propaedeutic to the standardization and application of the use of applications, processes, and devices that emerge from Revolution 4.0 to the investigation of the social world.

It is in this context that what we propose here is based on taking some of the central features of both social networks and digital and mobile devices as a basis for identifying, recording, analyzing, and interpreting information that allows understanding the current structuring of the social world.

Those applications that were created for mere social communication purposes can be used as instruments of inquiry, as research techniques at the service of a specific migration problem, for example. It is in this framework that digital research is social research through other means, by which a redefinition is required of both the research techniques and the standards of the processes that social research implies. Ethnography, observation, interview, survey, and the visual record are redefined from the fact that they are produced in a digital context, elaborated through digital instruments, and analyzed within the framework of the multimodal and multilevel convergence of the possibility of capturing the digital/mobile/virtual.

In this sense, this book makes it evident how Instagram allows capturing, through the production of photos, the expressive resources associated with a social network created to express the world through images but which in turn adds the use of video, interview, and observation.

In addition, it will be shown in another chapter how WhatsApp can be converted into a registration surface, an inquiry tool, and storage space. It will become clear how through this social network, researchers and subjects of the action can communicate at the moment that the action is unfolding, providing a new element in the definition of what it means to observe.

In another chapter, the book addresses the use of drones in research, from which the importance of having an overhead view of social relations will be pointed out. Seeing "from up", "overhead look", and "aerial view" are literally changing the perspective of observation on the world; the limitations and possibilities of drones make it possible to establish new perspectives for social research.

In the same direction, the theory and experience of digital ethnography will be made explicit as a social research technique where metaphorically the world fits in the researcher's computer, that is, a look at a society that includes the narratives of the subjects, videos of the subjects, photos of the practices, and all the forms of production and registration of reality that the same social subjects produce.

Through the use of certain applications, it is possible to perceive how, from digital social research, all available digital resources can be used as tools to build knowledge about emotions and to promote creativity and expressiveness. It is in this vein that finally, a space in the book is dedicated to the explanation of what we have come to call Digital Creative Experiences, which are the virtual/mobile version of our Expressive Creative Encounters using Zoom. Thus, a platform designed to "meet" becomes a space for experiences, where subjects can express the emotions they experience through memes, photos, stickers, drawings, etc.

It is evident that a set of possibilities has been confirmed for the Internet with its impact through social networks based on network applications, and the use of messaging in the era of the Smartphone; they become vehicles of research, surfaces of inquiry, and sources of the processes of double hermeneutics and epistemic surveillance for social research.

An aspect that also connects with the emergence of the virtual/mobile/digital world is the thematic of artificial intelligence (Williams, 2021), which we have addressed in Scribano and Mairano recently. A synthetic approximation of some of the axes addressed there could be the following:

> From a critical perspective of the sociology of body/emotions, the new millennium manifests the predatory expansion of capitalism on a planetary scale, and the consequent manifestation of a series of changes and transformations in social processes on a world scale; among them: the mobile/digital revolution that implies the large-scale increase in the use of the Internet and mobile devices, the reconfiguration of work in digital work and the new political economy of morality. One of the central effects of the relationship between Society 4.0, digital work and the social structuration process is the change in the politics of sensibilities, and with it the reconfiguration of the notions of space/time in the virtual/mobile/digital landscape.
>
> *(Scribano & Mairano, 2021, p. 229)*

If we focus on artificial intelligence, in recent years it has expanded and diversified. Today it is considered "a branch of science oriented towards the creation of intelligent machines with abilities to learn, adapt and act autonomously" (Sossa Azuela, 2020, p. 22). Scribano and Mairano go on to say the following:

> According to various versions, these machines become intelligent by being able to make appropriate decisions in uncertain circumstances, as well as having the potential to learn to improve their behaviour based on their experiences. Regarding the studies on AI, a considerable number of them have tried to conceptually delimit the social practices around the new technology.
>
> *(Scribano & Mairano, 2021, p. 229)*

In the framework described, it can be understood how AI presents various contributions, such as image recognition systems, virtual assistants, assisted driving, chatbots, robots, intelligent logistics applications, and transport processes, etc. But in the case that interests us most in this book that connects directly with the social media industry, AI is a key factor for "systematization/monitoring" of the data of millions of users of social networks such as Facebook, Twitter, and Snapchat, among others.

The entertainment industry is already used by providers such as Amazon and Netflix, which require the management of algorithms to present proposals for movies, programs, etc. It is possible to understand how these technological systems are applied to multiple tasks that modify our relationship with the world, based on machine learning, deep learning, natural language processing, algorithmic game theories, collaborative systems, automation of robotic processes, etc.

The book is dedicated to exposing how it is possible to systematize some "rules" for qualitative social inquiry in and through the virtual/digital/mobile world using the processes and applications created by its expansion on a planetary scale.

Through concrete examples of research carried out, the outstanding features of a qualitative look are presented that complement and investigate different paths to Big Data and all the quantitative strategies already widely used.

The proposal is based on underlining the central role of emotions in the process of social structuring and offering the devices, applications, and processes created in and from the virtual/digital/mobile world as instruments to observe them.

## I.3 Some Basic Questions and Assumptions

In the context described, among the many questions that arise, three are key to understanding this book, regarding the existence or not of Digital Emotions, the scope of the "virtual" in the context of the digital divide, and connection to ethics and consent in research in the digital world.

### *I.3.1 Digital Emotions*

This is not a book about the content of digital emotions understood as those that are produced, circulated, and reproduced in and through the virtual/mobile/digital life world but a work that presents tools from the social sciences to investigate this form of emotions.

As will be seen in Chapter 7 (and shown in each chapter of the book), it is unnecessary to establish the difference between the real and the virtual, because the world of virtual/mobile/digital life provides tools to know the world in general and to know oneself, and it is in this context that it is possible to sustain the existence of digital emotions.

In the first place, it is possible to verify what Giaxoglou and his colleagues call emotions of social networks, that is, elaborated by digital means and expressed through the "applications" of interaction:

> The socially mediated communication of emotion is intricately linked to the social textures of networking technologies, which include the affordances of persistence, replicability, scalability, and searchability (...) in an emerging culture of sharing (...). This means that existing views and definitions of emotion are not adequate and need to be complemented by understandings of networked contexts. In other words, theories of emotion become theories of networked emotion, that involves the mobilization of affect in online emotional cultures as a transmittable, spreadable, and

> self-contained resource, bringing out formerly privately shared emotions into online spaces and collective experience.
>
> *(Giaxoglou et al., 2017, p. 2)*

As can be found at various times in the book, the personal, the online surfaces, and the collective experiences appear here. This brings us to another controversial point, is there a sharp division between the living and the virtual? Chirico and Gaggioli in their study on the matter answer emphatically:

> Our findings indicated that the experiential profiles of exposure to natural environments in vivo and in virtuo were not significantly different, suggesting that virtual experience is a reliable model of the real one. Virtual simulation technologies are increasingly being applied in psychotherapy, tourism, museum exhibitions, training, and many other areas. In all these fields, the degree of similarity between the simulated real experiences plays a central role in shaping the value of the application. If confirmed by future studies, these findings indicate that emotions in a virtual situation are not less authentic than in a real situation, supporting the use of VR and simulation technologies in these areas. Finally, at the methodological level, these results suggest that VR provides an ecologically valid paradigm to study emotions in a laboratory.
>
> *(Chirico & Gaggioli, 2019, p. 6)*

The connections/disconnections between living, experience, and existence are similarly instantiation actions in "live" scenarios and "virtual" spaces that increasingly characterize Society 4.0. Both environments and experiences point in the direction of what Alinejad calls techno-emotional mediations with caregiving practices:

> Through an investigation of how family members who stayed "behind" in Romania use digital media to communicate with their loved ones abroad, I address this paper's central question of how transnational care is digitally mediated, suggesting how media scholarship might further enhance understandings of care in contemporary contexts of globalization. I conceptualize the long-distance emotional experiences I present in this paper as the techno emotional mediation of care, drawing on interview material gathered in Romania among the family members of those who emigrated from Romania under various circumstances. Romania has not only seen recent concomitant booms in both intra-EU migration and smartphone use, it also has a post-soviet history of massive domestic care labor migration to Southern European countries.
>
> *(Alinejad, 2021, p. 446)*

From the perspectives pointed out, as we will maintain in the book (especially in Chapter 1) and as we have written in other places (Scribano, 2019; Scribano & Lisdero, 2019), the life lived in Society 4.0 implies particular modalities of linking impressions, perceptions, and sensations and with it the configuration of emotions, emotional ecologies, and a particular politics of sensibilities.

### *I.3.2 Inequalities*

Deborah Lupton wrote about the digital age that "digital media technologies have become central to the lives of most people living in developed countries and increasing numbers of those in the developing world" (Lupton, 2019, p. 475).

The connections between emotions and the virtual/mobile/digital world are one of the central characteristics of the development of so-called Society 4.0 (or by some already 5.0). Entertainment from Netflix to Spotify; the practices of eating from food tech modality to the purchase of food and meals through platforms such as UberEATS or Deliveroo; the development of consumption through large companies such as Amazon, eBay, or Alibaba point out the intimate relationships between emotions, enjoyment, and technology. This is a world where people have access to the Internet and a life of virtual interactions using Facebook, instant messaging through mobile devices using applications such as WhatsApp, Telegram, or microblogging such as Twitter, and where applications such as Instagram, TikTok, and Tinder are used to express ideas, opinions, and emotions. Revolution 4.0 is characterized by the Internet of Things, where artificial intelligence, data mining, and the digitalization of production have permeated through computers, cell phones, and other mobile devices through a social structuration process. It is in this context that for ten years a virtual/mobile/digital world has been consolidated.

In recent years, and especially after the COVID-19 pandemic, the planetarization of capitalism, the world weight of digitalization, and the globalization of the "world of life 4.0" have accelerated the transformation of social relations in both the Global North and the Global South, giving clear signs of expansion.

In a report entitled "The future of work in South Africa Digitization, productivity and job creation" in 2019, the prestigious consultancy McKinsey argues that:

> In total, South Africa has the potential to create up to 4.5 million new jobs across many sectors as a result of productivity improvements, strategic policy implementation and the evolution of technology. We estimate that there could be a net gain of more than 570,000 jobs in the healthcare and social-assistance sector alone, and a net gain of more than 260,000 jobs in construction.
>
> *(Magwentshu et al., 2019, p. 8)*

China is a clear example of the world weight of digitalization and globalization of the world of life 4.0 and the consequences associated with it:

> According to the 2018 China Online Celebrity Economic Development Insight Report, "By May 2018, cyber celebrities with over 100,000 fans

> rose by 51 per cent from a year ago. Their total followers rose 25 per cent to 588 million". The boom in Internet celebrities has greatly influenced Chinese society. It already commands huge audiences, and it is likely that these will continue to grow. Internet celebrities have a huge influence and social impact on China, especially at the moral level. They set society's standards and moral direction and thus shape political sensibilities.
>
> *(Scribano & Jingting, 2019, p. 191)*

These processes of social structuring are generated within the framework of existing material inequalities that are compounded by well-known gaps and inequalities of gender, ethnicity, class, and age to which must be added the now very present digital inequalities:

> Women are very much underrepresented in AI and in the tech industry more broadly. A 2020 World Economic Forum report on gender parity suggests women account for only 26% of data and AI positions in the workforce. We need to get more women into AI.
>
> *(Firth-Butterfield and Ammanath, 2021)*

In the framework of a complex network, old and new inequalities share spaces with unexpected and "contradictory" expansions of the virtual/mobile/digital world. In this context, it is possible to take two very different examples to observe this, one in the African continent and the other in Latin America, that show at macro and micro levels the dissimilar consequences of the impacts of the virtual/mobile/digital world today.

The Briter Bridges Report (2021), based on measurements representing a combination of data available through online sources and information provided by investors, argues that start-ups operating in Africa raised at least $1.3 billion in 2020, emphasizing their growth and expansion.

On the other hand, in August of 2020, from the statements of the Vice President of the Argentine Republic Cristina Fernandez, 21-year-old musician L-Gante, with a school notebook and a very cheap microphone, caught political attention and jumped to fame after releasing "L-Gante Rkt" in collaboration with Papu DJ, which has gained more than 220 million views on YouTube.

The "world" and the "instruments" that this book deals with have emerged in the context of the 21st century where new inequalities are generated that overlap and connect with others given their massiveness and intersectional globalization.

### *I.3.3 Ethics and Consent in Research on the Digital World*

The strategies and methodological instruments proposed in this book must be inscribed in the respect and consideration of a post-intersectional, postcolonial, and non-speciesiste perspective, where, from the ontological to the procedural, it is elaborated under an epistemological surveillance that avoids all kinds of discrimination and manipulation of narratives, practices, and motivations, both of the researchers and of the people with whom the inquiry is shared.

In addition, the market, the state, and civil society are today concerned about digital ethics, the risks, and valuation mutations that come with the constitution of a Society 4.0 company. In this context, Simone Belko has given the following advice to ethically manage technology:

> Compliance not only focuses on legal aspects, but also on the social responsibility of the company's own products or services. Ethical design naturally adheres to legal requirements for the protection of the user, such as the "Privacy by Design" of the GDPR. (...) Freedom of choice. (...) It is a commonplace that clarity, simplicity, and intuitive operation make web interfaces easier to navigate. But often the orientation to the user's impulses for action (call-to-action) is confused with guided action and digital nudging. (...) Emotional security. A calm, safe environment promotes mindfulness and creates emotional safety so that the user can build trust. Rhythmic routines including pauses and an authentic learning environment contribute to disturbance-reduced grounding that favors concentration and individual mobilization. (...) Cultural diversity. One important factor is the adaptation of web interfaces, apps or online stores to regional and cultural characteristics. The focus here is on aligning design and product development more closely with the diversity of communities, rather than with artificial homogenization that does not reflect the real world.
>
> *(Belko, 2021)*

The digital research we propose here involves informed consent or is governed by the suggested rules of national and international associations, for example, the British Sociological Association:

> "Confidentiality is not required with respect to observations in public places, activities conducted in public, or other settings where no rules of privacy are provided by law or custom. Similarly, confidentiality is not required in the case of information available from public records".
>
> *(Papademas and IVSA, 2009: 254)*

> "Visual researchers may conduct research in public places or use publicly-available information about individuals (e.g. naturalistic observations in public places, analysis of public records, or archival research) without obtaining consent".
>
> *(Papademas and IVSA, 2009: 255)*

> "In the UK and the USA, anyone is allowed to take photographs in public places, even if the photo shows a private place"
>
> *(Rose, 2012: 334)*

> "There may be fewer compelling grounds for extending guarantees of privacy or confidentiality to public organisations, governments, officials or agencies than to individuals or small groups. Nevertheless, where guarantees have been given they should be honoured, unless there are clear and compelling public interest reasons not to do so".
>
> *(BSA 2017: 5; BSAVSSG, 2006: 6–7)*

> "unless consent has been sought, observation of public behaviour needs to take place only where people would 'reasonably expect to be observed by strangers'"
>
> *(BPS, 2007: 3)*

> Public Domain Mark 1.0 (Creative Commons): "This work has been identified as being free of known restrictions under copyright law, including all related and neighboring rights. You can copy, modify, distribute and perform the work, even for commercial purposes, all without asking permission".
>
> *(Creative Commons, 2016a)*
>
> *(BSA, 2020, p. 2)*

The International Association of Internet Studies analyzes the problem and provides, among others, the following reflections:

> Conceptual Issues: Ethical Frameworks and Concepts. As with IRE 1.0 and 2.0, a wide range of diverse ethical frameworks and concepts can be fruitfully brought to bear upon issues emerging within IRE 3.0. i.e., as helpful conceptual tools for analysing and, ideally, resolving ethical conflicts. These begin with utilitarianism and deontology, alongside virtue ethics, feminist ethics, and (feminist) ethics of care, which have become much more prominent in recent decades. These large frameworks are frequently tuned specifically to internet research issues. (...) Broadly, these frameworks address such foundational ethical norms and commitments as autonomy and freedom (especially in deontological ethics), along with the basic elements of IRE, such as informed consent and confidentiality. AIR members have also pointed to specific ethical topics such as accountability, trust, and transparency as also critical to good research practice and ethics – though not always easy to define or apply in praxis. Similarly, AIR researchers often highlight responsibility – towards oneself, one's institution, and the larger society, including returning some sort of benefit back to the communities under study.
>
> *(Shakti et al., 2020, p. 18)*

One of the keys to connecting with the people with whom our research experiences are shared that is reflected in this book is characterized by trust, consent, and the experience of the public and collective with respect for privacy and plurality. It is key that all readers be encouraged to take this into account when carrying out the necessary epistemological vigilance in each procedure.

## I.4 Book Content

The book consists of seven chapters and one introduction that reflect the intention of enabling a theoretical, epistemological, and methodological understanding of the proposed strategies under the assumption that such spheres of social knowledge must be made explicit when conducting social research.

Each chapter contains a) what is known about the subject of the chapter, b) the substance of an investigation carried out with the "technique" addressed in the chapter, and c) the central place that said strategy has in the capture of the sensations, emotions, and sensibilities.

The Introduction, Chapter 1, and Chapter 7 form three sides of the proposal so that the reader can connect all the chapters with the theoretical assumptions of the book and the epistemological view of digital emotions that is proposed.

### *I.4.1 Introduction*

As a starting point for the book, the introduction presents a) an approach to what can be understood as digital research, b) a characterization of the so-called Society and Revolution 4.0, c) the clarification of some basic assumptions of the text, which includes a reflection on digital emotions, inequalities, and issues related to ethics and consent in research on the digital world, d) the schematic presentation of the content of the book, and e) some anticipated conclusions.

### *I.4.2 Chapter 1. Bodies/Emotions and Virtual/Mobile/Digital Lifeworld*

As has been pointed out in the Introduction, there is currently no sharp division between the "real world" and the "digital world". This chapter aims to introduce the reader to the theoretical perspective that supports the methodological strategies offered in this book, introducing its basic theoretical and epistemological assumptions. To achieve this goal, it presents a) our approach to bodies/emotions sociology in a summarized way, b) a brief characterization of Society 4.0, and c) a synthesis of what I have worked on so far in creative/expressive social research, to explain in what sense what is presented in the book should be understood as a contribution to social qualitative research.

### *I.4.3 Chapter 2. Instagram, seeing to Believe: Soup Kitchen in Latin America*

This chapter aims to introduce readers to the world of Instagram from some of the qualities of the images produced on this application as a redefinition of feeling (oneself) and the image, emphasizing its potentialities as a modality of social inquiry. To achieve the aforementioned objective, proposed are: a) a first approach to Instagram, b) a synthesis of the digital ethnography of soup kitchens carried out during 2020 in 18 Latin American countries, c) the possible connections between knowing, living, and touching as features of Instagram images, opening a space to discuss the qualities of the current scopic regime, and d) concluding by asserting the need to ask ourselves about our *video touching* condition as producers of sensibilities that allow us to know/feel the world.

### I.4.4 Chapter 3. WhatsApp, Communicate, Register, Know: Argentinean Social Conflict and the March of Hondurans to the USA

The main objective of this chapter is to present a research experience using WhatsApp, especially from a methodological/epistemic/theoretical perspective. This motivation is accompanied by the conviction that the social sciences must deepen the evaluation of new forms of inquiry. In achieving the proposed, the following will be carried out: a) the reader is introduced to the outstanding features of the connections between WhatsApp and social research, b) two experiences of an investigation are described: The Everyday Gaze about the context of social conflict and hunger, and the caravan of Hondurans who migrated to the USA in 2018, c) some notes on the emotional ecologies found are presented, and d) some consequences and learnings are synthesized.

### I.4.5 Chapter 4. Politics and Love: Two Digital Ethnographies

Society 4.0 implies an increase in the life lived by subjects in mobile/digital/virtual settings and with this, the challenge for the social sciences is to systematize observation processes of that daily life. Traditional ethnography, observation, and various forms of participatory research have allowed the social sciences to have the necessary resources to think of new observation devices. Digital ethnography especially is presented as an inquiry device through which sensibilities and emotions are captured. This chapter outlines the central features of digital ethnographies: a) facilitating a conceptual approach that allows understanding the basic concepts of the device, b) synthesizing two examples of research carried out, and finally, c) it presents some theoretical and epistemological features of Digital Ethnography as a conclusion.

### I.4.6 Chapter 5. Drones: A New Way to Observe the Sensibilities on Social Interactions?

Look from up, look from an "aerial view" without climbing – flying is recent widespread activity of human beings. Drones are changing the possibilities of the way we see, look, and observe. This chapter proposes introducing readers to two features of the practices of seeing which the existence of drones directly impacts: a) the social practices associated with their uses and b) as vehicles for social research. To achieve this objective, the chapter is divided as follows: after the introduction, a) it makes explicit the connections between Society 4.0 and drones, b) it summarizes the various possibilities for the use of drones, c) it introduces some key aspects of the use of drones in social research, d) it presents a concrete example of research that uses drones, and finally e) it opens new analysis suggestions on the potential of the use of drones in social research.

The chapter aims to show the complexity involved in the use of drones and their ability to make possible a shared and plural view from a position usually associated with power but that can be redefined by the social sciences as a vehicle of inquiry and criticism.

### *I.4.7 Chapter 6. Digital Creative Experience: A Sensibility Capture Device*

The COVID-19 pandemic has led to new ways of social inquiry. In the context of what we have developed since 2009 as Expressive Creative Encounters, we carry out the task of adapting this device to capture sensibilities of the virtual/mobile/digital environment. This chapter seeks to make a first presentation of Digital Creative Encounters carried out in six countries of Latin America with young students of sociology in a situation of confinement due to the pandemic in 2020. To achieve the proposed objectives, the following exposition strategy has been adopted: a) the context of the "birth" of Digital Creative Encounters as creative/expressive devices is introduced, b) some features of the use of Zoom in social research is discussed, c) the components of Digital Creative Encounters are synthesized, d) some examples of Digital Creative Encounter drawings are shown, and e) finally some keys to understanding the usefulness of Digital Creative Encounters are outlined.

### *I.4.8 Chapter 7. Towards an Epistemology of the Digital Research of Emotions*

Every research strategy implies a connection with theoretical views and epistemological assumptions. This final chapter returns to the connections that exist in the emotional ecologies that have emerged in the previous chapters, emotions as texts, and the virtual/mobile/digital world that brings us closer to a hermeneutics of the practices of feeling. In this direction a) we reconstruct the "partial conclusions" of the tools and devices exposed in the framework of digital research on emotions, b) we present trust and consumption as key feeling practices to understand Society 4.0, and finally, c) we expose hope as an example of the implication of a critique of Society 4.0 within the framework of the epistemic features of emotions and their importance in the virtual/mobile/digital world.

## I.5 Some Anticipated Conclusions

From a general perspective, the book presented here can be said to contain a series of conclusions and questions that may open up new areas of possible research. In each case, these considerations are exposed first from the perspective of each proposed device and then from a more general perspective. It is important to emphasize that what is expressed here of an application or device does not mean that the others do not produce it but that, according to what is narrated in this book, it is connected more with one than with another.

Thinking about the use of WhatsApp as support, as an environment, or as a tool for inquiry, it can be said that WhatsApp allows a multimedia voice of expressiveness to be developed that, due to WhatsApp's ability to share audio, images, videos, and text messages, configures a scenario where emotions and sensibilities are performed and captured. In addition, WhatsApp is a way to capture a sensation the moment it is felt. Using WhatsApp allows feelings to be both expressed and recorded in various ways, which in turn makes it possible to observe critically how particular emotions are expressed at particular times.

WhatsApp implies an epistemology of the instant of showing and showing instantly; it is a portrait of the here and a narrative of the now. That is why the moment becomes key to what is expressed and what was intended to be expressed. A cognitive/affective moment is established by which emotions play the fundamental role of organizers of the world. From a more functional perspective, the application presented here clearly shows how choosing WhatsApp as a research tool allows the creation of international research teams and deterritorialized registries, which results in cognitive, learning, and collaboration benefits.

Instagram is the application where the image has a central place and clearly shows how seeing and making others see have a direct connection with knowing and feeling through a vehicle designed to impact the senses. It is in this direction that Instagram allows the reconstruction of the politics of the gaze, which anticipates the perception of the other by "making them feel" through the image. People seek to provoke emotions; they manufacture impressions for the perception of the other and themselves. It is because of this that the application becomes a suggestive device to capture emotions. In our experiences with Instagram as an instrument of inquiry, the maxim is concretized: "I see, then I feel… I feel, then I am", so it becomes especially important to incorporate the use of this type of application for social inquiry. From a functional perspective, it is very useful that through Instagram "stories", states and reels can be relieved of the traces of Politics of the Sensibilities throughout the "popular" themes of a given moment.

Beyond the logic and massive distrust of drones, these vehicles are new observation tools that can open very powerful spaces for the social sciences. Firstly, they can allow the possibility of collaborative expression against the politics of those who observe from the privileged top of a hierarchy; drones are machines that allow us to see everyone. Secondly, the use of drones allows the capture of possible disconnections between people, incorporating not only the zenith gaze but also the gaze after the encounter – an observation where the subjects "lose" the state of being co-present. Thirdly, the "performativity" of what is seen at a distance is verified, and the consequences of the action can be observed and recorded beyond the time/space un-anchoring that occurs between people when the action is finished. Functionally, drones are devices that allow recording to be digitized the moment it is captured, which is an advantage over other forms of image capture.

Zoom, like similar applications (Meet, Tennat, etc.) that have "revolutionized" the way of communicating, directly impacts the modality of experiencing a situation. From the old phone through to the arrival of Skype, the new applications allow large-scale synchronous group and collective interactions.

Similar to our proposal of Digital Creative Experiences, these applications allow us to capture experiences from digital feeling practices to producing encounters of experiences. Our experience is that they allow us to elaborate a hermeneutic of the face as an indication of emotions, and this transforms these applications into very effective instruments to capture these emotions.

Finally, Facebook as the "oldest" of these instruments, still maintains the power of being the first multimedia platform of expressiveness where much of the virtual/mobile/digital world "lives" for a large number of people. Facebook creates and maintains the feeling of being in the neighbourhood, of being with others waiting for exchange, and is presented as the "ideal" situation for digital ethnographies.

Particularly with Facebook but also generally in several of the applications that we have used, it is possible to see clearly how the rules of digital practices are elaborated to "translate" emotions. Some of the results of capturing emotions on this platform are having the feeling of being, sharing, and entering/leaving. From there, the new challenge of the metaverse is created.

This book should be considered as the first step in a long journey of exploring the close connections between sensibilities, emotions, and social research methodology. In the framework of what has been developed, the book ends with some schematic features of a political epistemology based on the hope that at least one possible connection between social research and the structuring of other possible worlds exists.

I cannot conclude this introduction without thanking all those who collaborated in one way or another in the preparation of this book, especially all those who are part of the Centre for Sociological Research and Studies (CIES) and the International Network of Sociology of Sensibilities (RedISS).

## Reference list


Alinejad, D. (2021). Techno-emotional mediations of transnational intimacy: social media and care relations in long-distance Romanian families. *Media, Culture & Society, 43*(3), 444–459.

Belko, S. (2021) Digital ethics in theory and practice, Mar 5. *MoreThanDigital*. Retrieved from https://morethandigital.info/en/digital-ethics-in-theory-and-practice/

Briter Bridges Report. (2021) *Africa's Investment Report 2021*. Retrieved from https://briterbridges.com/africainvestmentreport2021

BSA. British Sociological Association. (2020). *Ethics Guidelines and Collated Resources for Digital Research Statement of Ethical Practice Annexe*. Retrieved from https://www.britsoc.co.uk/media/24309/bsa_statement_of_ethical_practice_annexe.pdf

Chirico, A. & Gaggioli, A. (2019). When virtual feels real: Comparing emotional responses and presence in virtual and natural environments. *Cyberpsychology, Behavior, and Social Networking, 22*(3), 220–226. http://doi.org/10.1089/cyber.2018.0393

Firth-Butterfield, K., & Ammanath, B. (2021). 5 ways to get more women working in AI. World Economic Forum. Retrieved from https://www.weforum.org/agenda/2021/08/5-ways-increase-women-working-ai/

Giaxoglou, K., Döveling, K., & Pitsillides, S. (2017). Networked emotions: Interdisciplinary perspectives on sharing loss online. *Journal of Broadcasting & Electronic Media, 61*(1), 1–10. http://doi.org/10.1080/08838151.2016.1273927

Gratch, J., Lucas, G.M., Malandrakis, N., Szablowski, E., Fessler, E., & Nichols, J. (2015). GOAALLL!: Using sentiment in the World Cup to explore theories of emotion. In International Conference on Affective Computing and Intelligent Interaction (ACII), 898–903.

Lupton, D. (2019). Digital sociology. In Germov, J., & Poole, M. (eds.), *Public Sociology: An Introduction to Australian Society* (4th ed., pp. 475–492). Allen & Unwin.

Magwentshu, N., Rajagopaul, A., Chui, M., & Singh, A. (2019). *The Future of Work in South Africa Digitisation, Productivity and Job Creation*. McKinsey.

Marres, N. (2017). *Digital Sociology: The Reinvention of Social Research*. Polity.

McLuhan, M. (1964). *Understanding Media: The Extensions of Man*. Gingko Press.

Salganik, M. J. (2018). *Bit by Bit. Social Research in the Digital Age*. Princeton University Press.

Scribano, A. (2019). *Love as a Collective Action: Latin America, Emotions and Interstitial Practices*. Routledge.

Scribano, A. & Jingting, Z. (2019). Internet Celebrities Bodies/Emotions in China's Society 4.0. *Debats. Journal on Culture, Power and Society, 4*, 189–200. http://doi.org/10.28939/iam.debats-en.2019-15

Scribano, A., & Lisdero, P. (Eds.) (2019). *Digital Labour, Society and Politics of Sensibilities*. Palgrave Macmillan.

Scribano, A., & Mairano, V. M. (2021). Narratives, emotions and artificial intelligence: a reading of artificial intelligence from emotions. *SN Social Sciences, 1*, 229. https://doi.org/10.1007/s43545-021-00237-z

Shakti, F., Bechmann, A. Zimmer, A., Ess, C., & the Association of Internet Researchers. (2020). *Internet Research: Ethical Guidelines 3.0*. https://aoir.org/reports/ethics3.pdf

Sossa Azuela, J. H. (2020). *El papel de la Inteligencia Artificial en la industria 4.0*. Universidad Nacional Autónoma de México.

Williams, S. (2021). Artificial Intelligence in the new era. *International Journal of Innovative Science and Research Technology, 6*(4), 10–15.

Zhang, S., Wei, Z., Wang, Y. & Liao, T. (2018). Sentiment analysis of Chinese micro-blog text based on extended sentiment dictionary. *Future Generation Computer Systems, 81*, 395–403. https://doi.org/10.1016/j.future.2017.09.048

# 1

# BODIES/EMOTIONS AND VIRTUAL/ MOBILE/DIGITAL LIFEWORLD

## Introduction

There are different ways of exploring emotions depending on theoretical and methodological approaches: the recognition of emotions through images (Sharif & Khan, 2017), the emotional labour research from hospitality and tourism (Lee & Madera, 2019), a critic of the sociology of emotions around the "dimension of social" on affective turn context (Romeu, 2020), how Education Technology (EdTech) companies are deploying emotional artificial intelligence to quantify social and emotional learning (McStay, 2020), the place of synaesthesia as a realist process for urban research (Tzanelli, 2020), and study on cultural differences in mixed emotional experiences induced by stimuli conflict (Zheng et al., 2021).

Eduardo Bericat (2016), following an established classification, points out five main approaches to the sociology of emotions:

1. *Cultural theories* see emotions not as mere biological responses but as social feelings. These feelings are conditioned by the culture of a society (its norms, values, ideas, beliefs, etc.), emerge in the course of patterned social interactions and are learned through a socialization process (Gordon, 1981; Illouz et al., 2014; Robinson, 2014). Societies have an emotional culture, an emotional vocabulary, feeling rules and display rules, which define, for every situation and for every social position a subject occupies, what should be felt and how feelings should be expressed (Hochschild, 1979, 1983).
2. For *symbolic interactionist theories*, the identity of the self constitutes the dynamic behind emotional arousal. Individuals, at all times, try to confirm both the image they have of themselves (self-concept) and the particular identities through which they act in any specific social interaction (role identity).

DOI: 10.4324/9781003319771-2

3. *Ritual theories* argue "that focused interaction, which these theories refer to as ritual, is at the heart of all social dynamics. Rituals generate group emotions that are linked to symbols, forming the basis for beliefs, thinking, morality, and culture" (Summers-Effler, 2006, p. 135). Taking the sacrificial rituals of aboriginal cultures, Collins (1981, 2004) distinguishes between positive emotions and moral feelings, which, directed toward the group itself, shape social solidarity, and the positive emotions and trust that individual participants feel in the form of emotional energy (EE). According to Collins, individuals always seek to maximize their emotional energy in every social encounter.
4. *Structural theories* of emotions, whose initial formulation we owe to T. D. Kemper (1978), explain the type of emotion felt by actors in the course of social interaction, focusing on specific relational characteristics. According to Kemper, there are two basic relational dimensions: power and status. Actors with power, or who gain power in an interaction, experience positive emotions such as satisfaction, confidence, and security, while actors with a low level of relative power experience negative emotions such as fear. Actors with a high level of status, or to whom others give deference, will feel positive emotions such as pride, while those that lack status, or lose it, will feel negative emotions such as shame.
5. *Exchange theories*, developed by George C. Homans and Peter M. Blau, have also been used to explain the complex world of emotions (Lawler, 1999). Social interaction is a process in which actors exchange valuable resources in order to obtain an advantage or benefit. Individuals try to obtain rewards or avoid punishments by maximizing the utility of their behaviour and calculating costs and investments (Turner and Stets, 2005, p. 180). Individuals "feel good" (positive reinforcement) when rewards exceed costs and investments, and they "feel bad" (negative reinforcement) when they do not. But the intensity and type of emotions provoked by a social exchange depend on many other factors: the type of exchange (productive, negotiated, reciprocal, or generalized) (Bericat, 2016, p. 499–500).

As has been pointed out in the Introduction, there is currently no sharp division between the "real world" and the "digital world". This chapter aims to introduce the reader to the theoretical perspective that supports the methodological strategies offered in this book, introducing its basic theoretical and epistemological assumptions. To achieve this goal, it presents a) our approach to a bodies/emotions sociology (Scribano, 2017, 2018) in a summarized way, b) a brief characterization of Society 4.0, and c) a synthesis of what I have worked on so far in creative/expressive social research, to explain in what sense what is presented in the book should be understood as a contribution to social qualitative research.

## 1.1 Sociology of the Body/Emotions: A Perspective

What we know about the world, we know by and through our bodies. Perceptions, sensations, and emotions build a tripod that allows us to understand where sensibilities are founded. Social agents know the world through their bodies. Thus, a set of impressions impacts the ways subjects "exchange" with the socio-environmental context. Such impressions of objects, phenomena, processes, and other agents structure the perceptions that subjects accumulate and reproduce.

Perception, from this perspective, constitutes a naturalized way of organizing the set of impressions that are given by an agent. This weaving of impressions configures the sensations that "produce" what can be called the internal and external world: social, subjective, and "natural" worlds. Such configurations are formed in a dialectic tension between impressions, perceptions, and their results that give sensations the "meaning" of a surplus or excess. Therefore, it puts them closer and beyond such a dialectic. Sensations, as a result, and as the antecedent of perceptions, locate emotions as an effect of the processes of adjudication and correspondence between perceptions and sensations. Emotions, understood as the consequences of sensations, can be seen as a puzzle that becomes the action and effect of feeling something or feeling oneself. Emotions are rooted in the "state of feeling" the world that allows the sustainment of perceptions. These are associated with socially constructed forms of sensations. At the same time, organic and social senses enable what seems unique and unrepeatable, as are individual sensations, and elaborate on the "unperceived work" of incorporating social elements into emotions.

What we know about the world, we know through our bodies, what we do is what we see, and what we see is how we divide the world. In this "here-now", the devices for the regulation of sensations are installed. By such devices, the social world is apprehended and narrated, that is, from the expropriation that gave rise to the situation of domination in the first place. Sensations are distributed according to the specific forms of corporal capital.

Corporal capital consists of the living conditions of individuals located in the individual body, subjective body, and social body. The tension between individual, subjective, and social bodies is one of the keys that will allow a deeper understanding of the connections between geometries of the bodies and grammars of action, which are part of the neo-colonial domination in Latin America and the Global South.

The tension mentioned above makes more sense when joining the body's perspective with the view from sensations. A privileged form of connection between collective action and social fantasies and phantoms is constituted by accepting that the body is the *locus* of conflict and order. It is the place and "*topos*" of conflict where (much of) the logic of contemporary antagonisms passes through. From this point of view, we can observe the formation of a political economy of morality: forms of sensibilities, practices, and representations that put domination into words.

In this context, we understand that social bearability mechanisms are structured around a set of practices-made-body, orientated to a systematic avoidance of social conflict. The processes of displacement of the consequences of antagonism are presented as specular scenarios unpinned (disembedded) in space and time. These allow the acceptance that social life "is done" as is always done by the individual and society as a whole. Associated with this, devices for the regulation of sensations consist of processes of selection, classification, and the elaboration of socially determined and distributed perceptions. Regulation implies some tension between the senses, perceptions, and feelings that organize the particular ways of "seeing oneself in the world" and "appreciation in the world" that classes and subjects possess. Chains and cognitive-affective schemas that connect (and disconnect) social practices as narratives and worldviews made flesh are the processes that we characterize as ideological. The identified mechanisms and devices are a practical and procedural hinge where crossings between emotions, bodies, and stories instantiate. Systems' social bearability mechanisms do not operate either directly or explicitly as "attempted control", nor "deeply" as processes of focal points of persuasion. These mechanisms operate "almost unnoticed" in the porosity of custom, in the frames of common sense, through the construction of sensations that seem the most "intimate" and "unique" that every individual possesses as a social agent.

In this context, there are ways bodies can act, which is to say that they can act depending on social energies and social inertia. In other words, certain forms of action embody the social geometries of displacement and social inertia. In this process, seeing, smelling, touching, hearing, and tasting coalesce into possible sociability, indicating social devices for the regulation of sensations.

Sensations, as a result, and antecedent of perceptions, give way to emotions which can be seen as the manifestation of the action and effect of feelings. They are rooted in the states of feeling the world that build perceptions associated with socially constructed forms of sensations. Emotions are practices that transform the world that, based on a biography of sensations, challenge the person, producing recognition of bodily and affective states that involve them in all the modalities of their geometry. Emotions are affective cognitive tendencies that: a) imply a movement, an activity, and a modification of time/space, b) serve as maps to recognize the interaction situations, and c) allow the management of the effects of said interactions.

Consequently, the politics of bodies (i.e., the strategies that society accepts to offer a response to the social availability of individuals) is a chapter – and not the least important chapter – in the instruction manual of power. These strategies are tied and "strengthened" by the politics of emotions that tend to regulate the construction of social sensibility. The politics of emotions requires regulating and making bearable the conditions under which social order is produced and reproduced.

The forms of sociability and experience are strained and twisted as if contained in a Moebius strip, along with the sensibilities that arise from regulatory devices and the mechanisms mentioned above. The need to distinguish and link the possible relations between sociability, experience, and social sensibilities becomes crucial at this point. Sociability is a way of expressing how agents live and coexist interactively. Experience is a way of expressing the meaning gained while being in physical proximity with others, as a result of experiencing the dialogue between the individual body, the social body, and the subjective body, on the one hand, and the natural appropriation of bodily and social energies, on the other. For the body to be able to reproduce experience and sociability, bodily energy must be an object of production and consumption. Such energy can be understood as the necessary force to preserve the state of "natural" affairs in systemic functioning. At the same time, the social energy shown through the social body is based on bodily energy. It refers to the allocation processes of such energy as the basis of the conditions of movement and action.

Thus, sensations are distributed according to the specific forms of bodily capital, and the body's impact on sociability and experience shows a distinction between the body image, the body skin, and the body movement. The forms of sociability and experience are intertwined and twisted as if in a Moebius strip with the sensibilities that arise due to mechanisms of regulating sensation.

Social sensibilities continually update the emotional schemes arising from the accepted and acceptable norms of sensations. They near or distantiate the interrelationships between sociability and experience. Sensibilities are shaped and reshaped by contingent and structural overlaps of diverse forms of connection/disconnection among various ways of producing and reproducing the politics of the body and the emotions.

The politics of sensibilities are understood as the set of cognitive-affective social practices tending to the production, management, and reproduction of horizons of action, disposition, and cognition. These horizons refer to: a) the organization of daily life (day-to-day, vigil/sleep, food/abstinence, etc.), b) information to sort preferences and values (adequate/inadequate, acceptable/unacceptable, bearable/unbearable), and c) parameters for time/space management (displacement/location, walls/bridges, enjoyment). Interstitial practices nest in the inadvertent folds of the naturalized, naturalizing surface of the politics of the bodies and the emotions of neo-colonial religion. They are disruptions in the context of normativity.

In this context, three concepts become relevant: "practices of wanting", "feeling practices", and "interstitial practices". Feeling practices are those practices that involve heterogeneous sets of relationships between sensations and emotions. Interstitial practices are those social bondages that break the political economy of morality – which structures sensibilities. Practices of wanting involve the possible connections between hope, love, and enjoyment, and are social relations that link us to "doing with" the other. The bar (/) that we inscribe between bodies/emotions implies a sociologized allusion to its uses in psychoanalysis to show the separation/union, distance/proximity, and possibility/impossibility between objects/discourses that we grant to what has been thought of as separate, specific, and distant disciplinary subfields.

The gesture of retaking psychoanalysis as an "ally" of the interpretation of the social (long-standing in social theory) is plotted in our gaze/retranslation of critical theory (Marcuse, Fromm, etc.), from critical hermeneutics (Ricoeur) and ideological criticism (Žižek). A reflection on the questions that the aforementioned "alliance" opens up exceeds the intentions of this chapter. We leave it for consideration elsewhere, but it seems appropriate to rethink the current separation between the aforementioned traditions in numerous contemporary studies as impossible denial and/or constitutive suppression, which leaves us at the door of a set of theoretical analyses in favour of an imagined impossibility.

We precisely propose to see in this bar the moment of the beginning of writing about, of, and with the bodies/emotions as narratives that imply and "intersect" them: a) as a space from where rather than losing, the differences are recovered as part of a Moebius-type band, and b) as a designating operator of the spiral effect implied by the "beginning/step/end" relationship structured both in bodies and in emotions.

In what follows, the characteristics of Society 4.0 are exposed very succinctly as a basic context in which both the production of digital emotions and the strategies developed by the book must be inscribed.

## 1.2 Society 4.0: A Synthetic Overview

The last Ericsson consumer report, entitled "10 Hot Consumer Trends 2030", sustains that the consumers expect an Internet of senses:

> This vision is not only based on expected technological advances, but also on consumer research: urban early adopters expect that we will be using all of our senses online by 2030. Of those, 68 percent want to use at least 1 of 6 conceptual internet of senses applications we have asked about, and 81 percent are open to the idea overall. Of those who want an internet of senses, 40 percent see immersive entertainment as a main driver for this change; 33 percent think better online shopping will be key; and 31 percent think this change will come about due to the climate crisis. The big five tech companies along with industry-specific companies are expected to dominate and run roughly half of all Internet of senses services by 2030.
>
> *(Ericsson, 2022)*

The last online survey of McKinsey, one of the most famous and powerful consultant companies in the world, was conducted from January 19 to January 29, 2021, and garnered responses from 1,140 C-level executives, senior managers, and business unit, department, or division heads representing a full range of regions, industries, company sizes, and functional specialities. The results of the survey are very clear about the future of the digital economy:

> The pandemic has dramatically increased the speed at which digital is fundamentally changing business. Our previous survey showed that across key areas of the business model, companies' overall adoption of digital

> technologies had sped up by three to seven years in a span of months. The newest results show that this acceleration is also happening at the level of core business practices: what was considered best-in-class speed for most business practices in 2018 is now slower than average. And at companies with the strongest technology endowments, respondents say they are operating at an even faster pace. (…) But it's not only the pace of business that the COVID-19 crisis has fundamentally changed. According to the survey, many respondents recognize that their companies' business models are becoming obsolete. Only 11 per cent believe their current business models will be economically viable through 2023, while another 64 per cent say their companies need to build new digital businesses to help them get there.
>
> *(McKinsey, 2022)*

As it is easy to understand, consumers and companies agree on the deepening of a digital age as part of everyday life. The virtual/mobile/digital revolution implies transformations in the management of labour, social interaction, the production and storage of the different forms of power, also being affected by them, and under the umbrella of these modifications are developing new politics of sensibilities.

On this horizon, it is possible to see that 21st-century capitalism has started another trip worldwide. These are not now the journeys of Marco Polo, Colón, or Magellan: it is the entire edifice of science that is navigating an even more unknown world, one where much of the wealth of the future lies: our bodies/emotions. The journey is long; it has just begun, the surface is still unknown, and the "new silk" is human sensibilities.

Beyond the existing theoretical differences, the world of emotions is built with the social foundations of the body: we are what we eat, drink, and breathe, and in that sense, we are already colonized. Our bodies/senses/emotions are being occupied by transgenic foods, carbon dioxide pollution, flavoured waters, and hundreds of products created and tested on a molecular and nanoscale level that impact in various ways on our central nervous systems, our endocrine systems, and our immune systems.

Hundreds of ships sent by the "new navigators" seek the gold of the new Indians, take up the new silk routes, and traffic new flavours, textures, smells, colours, and sounds; following Montesquieu's advice, they elaborate the bases of a sweet trade between corporations and countries. The colonization of emotions, and colonized emotions, in the 21st century, have at least three paths of entry and production:

1. The search for the interpretation of the meaning of emotions with different strategies of identification, reading, and hermeneutics. The paths used range from surveys through artificial intelligence to reaching the application of sensors.

2. The construction of devices, robots, and mechanisms that reproduce and interpret sensations and cognitive-affective evaluations of emotions and sensibilities.
3. The design, elaboration, and implantation of interfaces, orthopaedics, implants, nano robots, and the establishment of mechanisms, processes, and substances that modify the structure perceptions/sensations/emotions/sen sibilities.

One of the most important aspects of the advent of companies in Society 4.0Industry 4.0 is the rapid development of social networks and the enormous growth of their commercialization and commercial value. In this framework, the interactions between the face-to-face social world, the virtual world, and the "mobile" world of cell phones and tablets have grown exponentially.

The Pew Research Center's "Social Media Use in 2021" report underlines that "a majority of Americans say they use YouTube and Facebook, while use of Instagram, Snapchat and TikTok is especially common among adults under 30" and maintains that:

> despite a string of controversies and the public's relatively negative sentiments about aspects of social media, roughly seven-in-ten Americans say they ever use any kind of social media site – a share that has remained relatively stable over the past five years.
>
> *(Pew Research Center, 2021, p. 3)*

Many authors argue that we are facing the Fourth Industrial Revolution and that this can be characterized by the consolidation of at least three factors: a) the appearance of Big Data as a resource for social diagnosis, b) the gig economy as evidence of the growth of deinstitutionalization, and c) the Internet of Things (IoT) as a new form of production and "management of sensibilities".

For its part, the use of Big Data analysis implies a) material surveillance of massive amounts of information about people and societies, b) Internet, social networks, and mobile interaction as a space for search, construction, and distribution of information, c) the digital dependence of the most dynamic sectors of the "real" economy, d) changes in the management of work and appropriation of the capital benefits, and e) the intimate relationship between the depredation of environmental assets and computer/digital assets.

Concerning the gig economy, it is possible to notice the following as central features: a) flexibility in the modalities of coordination of action, b) transformations in resources to guarantee competencies, c) the contingency of temporary and spatial links between the consumer and the producer, and d) the change of the means of payment for services and goods.

On the other hand, the IoT brings the following consequences: a) a new kind of "do it yourself" paradigm, 3) the redefinition of proximity/distance between the product and the producer, and c) changes in the relationship between "materials"/sensation. The increasingly important weight of the "cloud" as a virtual space for production, storage, management, and distribution of information must be added.

Indeed, among the many factors that converge for modifying the modes of work management, knowledge, and production at present, the cloud is the most important one. This is so since a) it is a virtual space designed to improve collaborative work, b) it allows the inequalities of access to expensive hardware to be obviated, and c) it promotes a more "agile" information management.

Another feature of the connection between Society 4.0 and labour is the so-called sharing economy, as maintained by Parente and his colleagues:

"The popularized 'sharing economy' term has been used frequently to describe different organizations that connect users/renters and owner/providers through consumer-to-consumer (C2C) (e.g., Uber, Airbnb) or business-to-consumer B2C) platforms, allowing rentals in more flexible, social interactive terms (e.g., Zipcar, WeWork)" (Parente et al. 2018, p. 53).

> "Collaborative consumption" and the "access-based economy" are other ways to identify a set of economic interactions based on the Internet as a platform and imply countless social transformations. One of these changes is consumption and consumers' new and stronger role in shaping economic interactions. In some way, these interactions modify the practices of having, possessing and using under the influence of the Internet and the time-space resignification that this implies. The "experiences of using" confront the perceptions about what it means to be an owner. In the aftermath of the global financial crisis beginning in 2008, consumers sought other means of gaining access to products and services aside from the burdens of ownership. A new economic model, known as the sharing economy or collaborative consumption, emerged, which integrated collaboration, technology, and the desire to be more efficient with products and services.
>
> *(Davidson et al., 2017, p. 364)*

The aforementioned processes intersect and interact with the expansion of the redefinition of institutions, as in the case of Uber, where one can observe a flexibilization, "liberalization", and resignification of state controls. In the same direction, it is possible to verify the growing impact of artificial intelligence in its different applications, such as chatbots, robots, drones, and other objects/processes linked to the IoT, and the modifications that this involves for everyday life.

In this Society 4.0, there is an important transformation of the political economy of morality, the politics of sensibilities, and the political economy of the truth associated with it. The structure of the political economy of morality accompanies the changes in the political economy of truth. It modifies the processes accepted to produce the truth, the criteria to accept perception as true, and the specialized areas to "guarantee" the truth.

The processes to obtain the truth move away from the traditional scientific procedures and toward logic, articulated around sensibilities and emotion. From the different forms of empathy, perception, and sensations of "capture", through intelligent regimes of emotional regulation, to alternative spiritualities, all are crossed and articulated as possible ways of reaching the truth.

Thus, socio neurology, the informative layout of haptic systems, fuzzy logic, body/machine interfaces, nanotechnology, genetic design, and artificial intelligence are some of the scientific procedures of the 21st century that "help" new ways of obtaining the truth. As instruments designed to "see things happening", drones "stretch" the current paradigm of sensibility, playing the role of witnesses that reproduce reality from a distance.

What is sustained up to now is more complex if we bear in mind that Society 4.0, among many other things, has transformed the potential of communicating through photographs, videos, and audio expressed on cell phones and smartphones.

What also brings its use as a technique to record, portray, and interpret the world, as argued by Lansen and Garcia (2015) in their study of photography, self-pornography, and social networks is the following:

> The contemporary practices of digital photography are connecting sociability, the "make-body" and subjectivity, especially with the convergence of digital cameras, mobile phones and social networks (...) The ubiquity of cameras and the growing exhibition exchange of images online reveal changes in the uses and meanings of everyday photographic practices. Enjoyment and experimentation are common features of camera phones and the use of digital cameras, which are similar in their uses for erotic purposes. These changes are possible thanks to the ease of digital production and the low cost of production for individuals.
>
> *(Lansen & García, 2015, p. 717)*

Precariousness, massification, instantaneity, and digitization of daily life are practices that consolidate the era of a new "politics of touching" and diverse "politics of seeing", and work is a space where these processes are rapidly and strongly evident.

In the scenery of the globalization of normalized societies in the immediate enjoyment through consumption, the processes of classification and qualification of touch are modified. Thus, a renewed "politics of touching" assembles different (and diverse) geometries of the bodies deployed in virtual environments and by digital resources. In the same vein, the proximity and distance between gaze, seeing, and observing are transformed on the digital horizon. Passing from augmented reality to the arrival of drones in daily life, we see modification and the appearance of a new form of "politics of seeing". Both the new "politics of touching" and diverse "politics of seeing" have a major impact on redefining the "world of work": "new" environments, resources, processes, and goals have been created, and with them, the labour and workforce are transformed.

In the remainder of the chapter, creativity, digital environment, social research, and emotion are linked to try and provide a horizon of understanding for the rest of the book.

## 1.3 Qualitative Social Research and Emotions

Several proposals guide the social research of emotions and the digital, but not so many propose to investigate digital emotions from a qualitative perspective. On emotions, the book edited by Flam and Kleres (2015) stands out, which offers a varied "menu" of possibilities, that of Camila Baker (2018) on smartphones, expressiveness, and performances; on the so-called digital humanities by Iewis et al. (2018), or the already classic contribution on the digital/virtual by Fielding (2017).

The proposals we make in this book are part of a long history of connections between creativity, expressiveness, emotions, and qualitative social research.

The expressiveness of social subjects has always been a controversial issue for the social sciences because nobody can "live within the other". But the "development" and "improvement" of qualitative social research strategies incorporating the "expressiveness' capture technologies" in a progressive yet steady way have been able to bridge the gap between what the researcher sees and what the subject expresses (Given, 2006; Kanstrup, 2002). From the traditional use of recording devices to the digital video camera, social scientists have been attempting to expand the capabilities of "apprehending" the social world and the voices of the people who build it (McGettigan, 1998; Penn-Edwards, 2004; McNaughton, 2009). Considering "participant observation" to the use of "theatre" and "dance" (Chakravorty, 2004; Malo, 2009), there are many strategies of inquiry that have been able to capture in an ever-improving way the indeterminable and expectable performance of subjects in social interactions. In this work, creativity is taken as a starting point to produce expressive experiences where individuals "share" and interpret, both with the researcher and with others, in particular social conditions of existence, their sensations and emotions. The creativity of human beings is a recurrent issue for social sciences (Bielsk, 2010).

By experiencing creativity as potency to capture and transform the world, qualitative inquiry ruptures and builds renewed paths to see the world with others and along with those involved in research. As they create, subjects inscribe different ways to express their emotions and sensations on multiple surfaces. If creativity is used as logic to inquire about what emerges from subjects and what is expected and "interests" the researcher, they become aspects that are mutually put in tension. These "findings" are transformed into a knot in which what the researcher is looking for and what the subjects "do" become articulated. Expressiveness is just making explicit what was implied, it is a de-wrapping action, a de-compression. In expressiveness, the tacit (what is assumed according to the "social bearability mechanisms" and "regulatory regimes of the sensations") manifests itself, it becomes present. At the same time, expressing oneself is a vehicle to disarm the "packaging" of class habitus, to get off what was wrapping and put it in connection with what was wrapped. Moreover, the expressiveness of subjects unpacks what was "tight", "concentrated" in the silent yet systematic differential appropriation and uses of the word as the only way of speaking.

This section intends to synthesize the methodological context in which the digital strategies proposed in the book must be inscribed. It is important to consider how the qualitative perspective of digital social research connects strongly with social research based on the creativity/expressiveness strategy on which we have been working for more than 20 years.

To achieve this objective, this section outlines: a) some of the creative/expressive research devices we have been using, and b) a fundamental methodological element that is explicit, such as the "units of experience" as a central component of the observation of emotions.

### *1.3.1 Research Based on Creativity and Expressiveness: A Way to Understand Emotions*

This book is the result of a long process of experimentation in special qualitative inquiry strategies in which the devices and tools described in it must be inscribed from a multi-method perspective and an intersectional, non-speciesist, and post-colonial ethics.

As developed in more detail in Chapter 6, since the end of the last century, I have explored the potentiality of the connection between qualitative social research and social research based on creativity/expressiveness. In the past decade, based on a set of experiences acquired in empirical research, I proposed the application of what I called "expressive creative encounters", in a paper entitled "Expressive Creative Encounters: a sociological research strategy of emotions" (Scribano, 2013), in which creativity is the starting point to produce experiences through which subjects "share" and "interpret" their inquiries from their social world, sharing said inquiries with the researcher.

Continuing with the motivation of connecting creativity and expressiveness, we proposed the "dance interviews" which consist of replacing the legacy of the in-depth interview and modifying the way of asking and answering. Thus, the researcher asks and the interviewee moves/dances from where they seek to capture the moments of expression that exceed the word. The aim is to explore another language system where the interviewer and the interviewee collaborate in the hermeneutics of movement as a way of expressing emotions.

Along the same lines, we created and applied what we call "eating experiences", where eating practices and commensality experiences were used. Here, the connections between colours, flavours, and textures of food with the personal, family, and collective history of the participants were explored. The device is organized around a shared meal of six people who start by identifying what they are eating with their eyes covered and come to associate the colours of the dishes with the sensations and emotions they experience.

Returning to the search for the potentialities of the interview, we proposed a modality that we call "sound dialogues", which consists of rehearsing a question/answer mechanism through sound/music/noise. The interviewer asks and the interviewee responds by producing sound. The potential of sound as a vehicle to express emotions is the central axis of the tool, always appealing to the first hermeneutic of the interviewee as a basic understanding of sensations and emotions.

### *1.3.2 Units of Experience: Observation, Registration, and Emotions*

In various works, we have been proposing alternatives to capture the complex relationships between creativity, expressiveness, sensations, and emotions.[1] Said alternatives are efforts to trace some paths that can be used to "observe", "record", "analyze", and "interpret" how subjects express their emotions when they perform creative acts. The quotation marks in the four moments of the inquiry accentuate the indeterminate nature of these moments and the complexity that they imply, plus the difficulties of continuing to call them that when they specifically refer to a possible look at sensibilities.

It is precisely in the superposition of the aforementioned complexities that the problem (and our proposal) of the units of experiences on a methodological topic of relevance today arises.

The proposal that has been presented, as we have already indicated in other places, implies moving from the dichotomy unit of observation – a unit of analysis to what we refer to as "unit(s) of experience". The three "types of units" must be understood as permanent tension and mutual self-involvement, only emphasizing the urgency of redirecting perception to a hiatus that opens between analysis and observation when it comes to the expressiveness of action. The unit of experience is thought of as a node through which the experience that the chromaticities of the distances and proximity between experience and expressiveness imply is vectorized. A node that makes it possible to identify and systematize the set of emotional overlaps that occur in an expressive act.

Trying to capture expressiveness involves a (dialectical) slippage where between what, to whom, and from whom it is expressed makes a "paradigm" play that transcends the metaphor of the eye. A paradigm of expressiveness is played in language games that rotate and intertwine around colours, movements, sounds, and the fluidity of the action.

The aforementioned "paradigm" involves two pairs of dialectical frameworks. The first goes from the impression, goes through the affection, and reaches the senses. The second opens in the face, and goes through the dramaturgical presentation to arrive at the presupposition (what is taken for granted), the gesture. Neither the first nor the second pair of lattices "maintain" a linear economy of causality, they only "appear thus in the perceiving" of the complex, indeterminate, and chaotic experience.

Now, how to discover/capture units of experience? To answer this question, and as was anticipated, in principle the problems of analysis and validity will be left aside and we will concentrate on the modes of records. Given this caveat, the question is re-located in the following way: how is it possible to register units of experience? Here two possible routes are advanced.

In the attempt to grasp it from the experience, the register of the experience of the expression of the others is a how to *do (it)*. The paths of recording, among others, the usual-unusual dyadic relationships, material-significations, armed-disassembled sensations that occur in creativity, expressiveness, and revelation of being (becoming) visible that suppose the locus of the photo, dance, theatre, etc.

The how "I register", assuming that it is taken for granted that the objectives and the expected results of the research in themselves mark the perception in its theoretical load and of what is in it of epistemic violence, can begin to be solved in the way that follows: a) the space of "inter-action" between what is in the lived experience of showing, showing (us), and showing (oneself) should be recorded, b) on the other hand, it is necessary to note the complexity as a "dramaturgical" situation (*sensu* Goffman) that exists in the "act of expression/creation", c) how, from where, with whom, and what do the expressions being registered have, d) it is also important to emphasize the ability to record expressiveness "silences", and e) it is necessary to recover the "plot" of the expressiveness of the sensations experienced in the emotions provoked by the modes of expressiveness.

Creativity/expressivity and experience shape the moments of the urgency of transformation of both the procedures and what must be recorded in the investigation of emotions in the mobile/virtual/digital world. This book has been written on the horizon of a view on bodies/emotions, the diagnosis of Society 4.0, and the tradition of creative/expressive social research, reviewed here; in any case, in the following chapters, the specific assumptions for each strategy will be explicit.

## 1.4 Digital Emotions and Social Research

In this section, some ways of considering digital emotions are synthesized as a horizon of understanding the next chapters.

From a schematic perspective, it is possible to assume that there are three spheres of social interaction that "clarify" the place of digital emotions today: their place in emotional contagion, their impact on creativity, and their connection with the Internet of Things and robotics.

Goldenberg and Gross (2020) have pointed out the existence of the contagion of digital emotions and how exposure to digital media facilitates such a contagion. If there is digital contagion, there is a digital mode of emotion that is what this book supposes and the devices presented produce. In this sense, Goldenberg and Gross expose how people spend more and more time in digital media, moments during which they are exposed to the emotional expressions of others, and which can cause their emotional expressions to become more similar to those of others. A distinction between the contagion of digital and non-digital emotions is that the contagion of digital emotions is a contagion of emotions mediated. Within the framework of what was developed by Goldenberg and Gross, this book reflects, in various places, how the participants in the research presented experience such mediation.

A very interesting aspect of the relationships between people in the research that the book presents is how they are challenged and unnoticed build an emotional interaction. Kramer et al. (2014) have long shown how emotional states can be transferred to others through emotional contagion, which leads people to experience the same emotions without them noticing. These authors argued that through laboratory experiences, it could be said that emotional contagion is adequately shown and that these results also indicate that the emotions expressed by others on Facebook influence our own emotions, which constitutes experimental evidence of large-scale contagion through social networks.

A second element that recognizes the existence of digital emotions in the sense indicated in this book is that of the creativity subject that Pérez-Fuentes and his colleagues clearly express in their article "Self-Expressive Creativity in the Adolescent Digital Domain: Personality, Self-Esteem, and Emotions". In their article they argue:

> Although self-expressive creativity is related to cyberbullying, it can also reinforce strengths that contribute to positive adolescent development. Our study concentrated on the relationships between personality traits and self-expressive creativity in the digital domain in an adolescent population. For this, we analysed the effect of self-esteem and emotional intelligence as assets for positive development related to personality traits and self-expressive creativity.
>
> *(Pérez-Fuentes et al., 2019, p. 1)*

In a very different sense, Rolbiecki et al. (2019) have explored the problem of bereaved families through an exploratory study of digital storytelling as grief intervention. They systematize their findings as follows:

> Themes from the data also revealed that participation in Digital Storytelling affected participants in these ways: (a) the writing and verbalization of the script helped participants organize their thoughts and emotions about the loss, (b) having the space to share with a collective group encouraged confidence in their ability to discuss their feelings with others, and (c) the final product served as a source of closure for participants.
>
> *(Rolbiecki et al., 2019, p. 1)*

It is important here to emphasize how the people who participate in our research on emotions through the strategies outlined in this book always express their gratitude for the opening of a space for the expression of emotions.

Finally, the connection between emotions and emotional intelligence and the automation of life throughout the digital, Internet of Things, and robotic is a basic pillar to comprehend the production context of the inquiry devices that this book contains.

For example, Toichoa Eyam and his colleagues in their work "Emotion-Driven Analysis and Control of Human-Robot Interactions in Collaborative Application", express the following:

> Consequently, the collaborative robots (Cobots) have been created to allow physical interaction with the human worker. However, these cobots still lack recognizing the human emotional state. In this regard, this paper presents an approach for adapting cobot parameters to the emotional state of the human worker. The approach utilizes the Electroencephalography (EEG) technology for digitizing and understanding the human emotional state. Afterwards, the parameters of the cobot are instantly adjusted to keep the human emotional state in a desirable range which increases the confidence and the trust between the human and the cobot.
>
> *(Toichoa Eyam et al., 2021, p. 1)*

An emotion unfolds in a time and a space using the body and is produced to be understood by the other.

Emotions can be anchoring or blur the relationship between time and space, that is, emotions can be awakened after going to look for a relationship: a face-to-face relationship with a person, an object, or a process, in which case between human beings will always be a face-to-face relationship.

This connection or disconnection of time and space will be mediated by different disembedding vehicles. The first is the face-to-face relationship, the second is the audience relationship, and the third is the relationship of disembedding through technological means that has two forms: a) the capacity for dialogue, and b) the transmission and listening of emotions.

In the last case of the technological media, we have to analyze the advent of the production, transmission, and experience of digital emotions. We will call digital emotions those that are produced, communicated, and reproduced through digital media, transforming the time-space of response to that emotion.

Digital emotions, as emotions, imply four moments: a) the moment of reproduction of saying and transmission of what one should usually feel in front of an object/a process/a person, b) the moment of implication, which is the level of personal commitment to what the practice involves, c) the cognitive moment that refers to the knowledge of the body movement, and the cognitive-affective states that are being experienced, and d) the moment of transformation of the responses to that emotional communication to which subjects are registered, which makes these become real and caused by those emotions.

A transformation in Revolution 4.0 has been the channels of emotional production: firstly, the audio-visual expansion, and secondly, the multiplicity of objects produced to generate emotions by digitizing processes, animated, and non-animated people and/or objects.

The mobile/virtual/digital world concentrates to a large extent on producing mass communication of specific means to generate emotions. The digital world is the result and the geometry of the digitized person. This is the individual, actor, agent, subject, and author, who meet from their characteristics in a space that allows a very wide versatility to convert these five sides of this geometry into bands of a Moebius strip, whose connections multiply and open up in numerous ways. In this way, digital emotion is based on the transformation of the haptic system, the modification of the sensibility of the skin body associated with the politics of sensations (view, touch, move), and the transformation of hermeneutic schemes to transmit emotional narrations.

The following chapters try to present to the reader synthetically the main characteristics of various strategies and devices to investigate digital emotions in digital environments.

## Note

1 *Cf.* Scribano (2008a, 2008b, 2008c).

## References


Baker, C. (2018). *New Directions in Mobile Media and Performance.* Routledge.

Bericat, E. (2016). The sociology of emotions: Four decades of progress. *Current Sociology, 64*(3), 491–513.

Bielsk, P. (2010). Book review: "Method meets art. Arts-based research practice by patricia leavy". New York – London: The Guilford Press, 2009. *Qualitative Sociology Review, VI*(3), 115–117.

Chakravorty, P. (2004). Dance, pleasure and Indian women as multisensorial subjects. *Visual Anthropology, 17,* 1–17. https://doi.org/10.1080/08949460490273988

Davidson, A., Reza Habibi, M., & Larochec, M. (2017). Materialism and the sharing economy: A cross-cultural study of American and Indian consumers. *Journal of Business Research, 82,* 364–372.

Ericsson. (2022). *10 Hot Consumer Trends 2030.* Retrieved from https://www.ericsson.com/en/reports-and-papers/consumerlab/reports/10-hot-consumer-trends-2030

Fielding, N. G. (2017). *The SAGE Handbook of Online Research Methods.* Sage.

Flam, H., & Kleres, J. (2015). *Methods of Exploring Emotions.* Routledge.

Given, J. (2006). Narrating the digital turn: Data deluge, technomethodology, and other likely tales. *Qualitative Sociology Review, II*(1), 54–65.

Goldenberg, A., & Gross, J. J. (2020). Digital emotion contagion. *Trends in Cognitive Sciences, 24*(4), 316–328. https://doi.org/10.1016/j.tics.2020.01.009.

Iewis, I., Tai, T., & Rheams, D. (eds.). (2018). *Research Methods for the Digital Humanities.* Palgrave.

Kanstrup, A. (2002). Picture the practice: Using photography to explore use of technology within teachers work practices. *Forum: Qualitative Social Research, 3*(2). https://doi.org/10.17169/fqs-3.2.856

Kramer, A. D., Guillory, J. E., & Hancock, J. T. (2014). Experimental evidence of massive-scale emotional contagion through social networks. *Proceedings of the National Academy of Sciences, 111*(24), 8788–8790. https://doi.org/10.1073/pnas.1320040111.

Lansen, A., & García, A. (2015). "...But I haven't got a body to show": Self-pornification and male mixed feelings in digitally mediated seduction practices. *Sexualities, 18*(5/6), 714–730.

Lee, L., & Madera, J. M. (2019). A systematic literature review of emotional labor research from the hospitality and tourism literature. *International Journal of Contemporary Hospitality Management, 31*(7), 2808–2826.

Malo, E. M. (2009). Perform strikes. A case study. *Qualitative Sociology Review, (VI)*, 29–49.

McGettigan, T. (1998). Reflections in an unblinking eye: Negotiating identity in the production of a documentary. *Sociological Research Online, 3*(1), 17–28.

McKinsey. (2022). *The New Digital Age: Rethinking Strategy for the Postpandemic Era.* Retrieved from https://www.mckinsey.com/business-functions/mckinsey-digital/our-insights/the-new-digital-edge-rethinking-strategy-for-the-postpandemic-era

McNaughton, M. J. (2009). Closing in on the picture: Analyzing interactions in video recordings. *International Journal of Qualitative Methods, 8*(4), 27–48.

McStay, A. (2020). Emotional AI and EdTech: Serving the public good? *Learning, Media and Technology, 45*(3), 270–283. https://doi.org/10.1080/17439884.2020.1686016

Parente, R. C., Geleilate, J. M. G., & Rong, K. (2018). The sharing economy globalization phenomenon: A research agenda. *Journal of International Management, 24*, 52–64.

Penn-Edwards, S. (2004). Visual evidence in qualitative research: The role of videorecording. *The Qualitative Report, 9*(2), 266–277.

Pérez-Fuentes M. D. C., Molero Jurado, M. D. M., Gázquez Linares, J. J., Oropesa Ruiz, N. F., Simón Márquez, M. D. M., & Saracostti, M. (2019). Self-expressive creativity in the adolescent digital domain: Personality, self-esteem, and emotions. *International Journal of Environmental Research and Public Health, 16*(22), 4527. https://doi.org/10.3390/ijerph16224527.

Pew Research Center. (2021). *Social Media Use in 2021.* April 2021. www.pewresearch.org

Rolbiecki, A. J., Washington, K. T., & Bitsicas, K. (2019). Digital storytelling as an intervention for bereaved family members. *Omega: Journal of Death and Dying, 82*(4), 570–586. https://doi.org/10.1177/0030222819825513.

Romeu, V. (2020). Notes for a critique to the program of the sociology of emotions. *Konfrontasi Journal: Culture, Economy and Social Changes*, 7(1), 67–76. https://doi.org/10.33258/konfrontasi2.v7i1.98

Scribano, A. (2008a). *El Proceso de Investigación Social Cualitativo.* Prometeo.

Scribano, A. (2008b). Re-tomando las sensaciones: Algunas notas sobre los caminos expresivos como estrategia para la investigación cualitativa. In Ayala Rubio, S. (coord.), *Experiencias y reflexiones desde la investigación social* (pp. 103–123). CUCEA, Universidad de Guadalajara.

Scribano, A. (2008c). Conocimiento Social e Investigación Social en Latinoamérica. In Cohen, N., & Piovani, J. I. (comps.), *La metodología de la investigación en debate* (pp. 87–117). Eudeba - Edulp.

Scribano, A. (2013). *Encuentros Creativos Expresivos: una metodología para estudiar sensibilidades.* Estudios Sociológicos Editora.

Scribano, A. (2017). *Normalization, Enjoyment and Bodies/emotions: Argentine Sensibilities.* Nova Science Publishers.

Scribano, A. (2018). *Politics and Emotions.* Studium Press.

Sharif, O., & Khan, R. (2017). A literature review on emotion recognition using various methods. *Global Journal of Computer Science and Technology, XVII*(0.1), 24–28.

Toichoa Eyam, A., Mohammed, W. M., & Martinez Lastra, J. L. (2021). Emotion-driven analysis and control of human-robot interactions in collaborative applications. *Sensors, 21*(14), 4626. https://doi.org/10.3390/s21144626.

Tzanelli, R. (2020). Synaesthesia and the mobile city. In Büscher, M., Freudendal-Pedersen, M., Kesselring, S., & Grauslund Kristensen, N. (eds.), *Handbook of Research Methods and Applications for Mobilities* (pp. 382–397). Edward Elgar.

Zheng, W., Yu, A., Li, D., Fang, P., & Peng, K (2021). Cultural differences in mixed emotions: The role of dialectical thinking. *Frontiers in Psychology, 11*, 538793. https://doi.org/10.3389/fpsyg.2020.538793

# 2

# INSTAGRAM, SEEING TO BELIEVE

## Soup Kitchen in Latin America

### Introduction

The chapter aims to introduce readers to the world of Instagram from some of the qualities of the images produced on the said network as a redefinition of feeling (oneself) and the image, emphasizing its potentialities as a modality of social inquiry.

To achieve the aforementioned objective, proposed is: a) a first approach to Instagram, b) a synthesis of the digital ethnography on soup kitchens carried out during 2020 in 18 Latin American Countries, c) the possible connections between knowing, living, and touching as features of Instagram images, opening a space to discuss the qualities of the current scopic regime, and d) concluding by asserting the need to ask ourselves about our *video touching* condition as producers of sensibilities that allow us to know/feel the world.

Mobile communication devices (from cell phones to tablets) have become spaces for production, editing, and a vehicle for storing images. Based on easily accessible and manageable programs, the owners of the aforementioned devices have become *image makers*. Instagram was born and globalized in the context of the convergence of these trends: the mass use of social networks, Revolution 4.0, and the emergence of the *image maker*. This chapter shows how Instagram is both a research surface and instrument of inquiry.

### 2.1 Instagram: An Approach

Instagram was created in 2010, and its brand name alludes to three factors that constitute its distinctive features: the allusion to the instant (insta) of the Polaroid camera (the format of the photos and the filters that the program takes as a reference), the sensation of drawing a graph, grammar, drawing (gram), and the communicative power of the telegram.

DOI: 10.4324/9781003319771-3

In the context of Society 4.0 and with the massive connection between *image makers*, a set of practices is distinguished that is typical of social networks in general (digital marketing, charity campaigns, policies, etc.) and others that have been consecrated and/or consolidated thanks to Instagram.

Among the previous practices alluded to, we want to emphasize two here: instafame and instagratification, both very clear examples of the connections between seeing/touching/feeling (which we develop in the next section) that Instagram carries. One of the most interesting processes that is evident on Instagram is what Marwick has called *Instafama*, which implies the massive popularity of "ordinary" people who have become celebrities.

Both Graeme Turner (2004) in *Understanding Celebrity* and Theresa Senft (2008) in her *Camgirls: celebrity and community in the age of social networks* had anticipated the multiplication of famous characters produced by the mass media and the Internet; from reality shows to the popularity of live webcams, people became characters in the format of massive and ephemeral celebrities.

Taking the model of the Hollywood celebrity in aesthetic, narrative, and even physical terms, the "instant famous" make the image their language and grammar in search of followers. In this context, Marwick declares:

> I argue that Instagram represents a convergence of cultural forces: a mania for digital documentation, the proliferation of celebrity and microcelebrity culture, and conspicuous consumption. Instafame demonstrates that while microcelebrity is widely practiced, those successful at gaining attention often reproduce conventional status hierarchies of luxury, celebrity, and popularity that depend on the ability to emulate the visual iconography of mainstream celebrity culture. This emulation calls into question the idea that social media are an egalitarian, or even just a more accessible way for individuals to access the currency of the attention economy.
>
> *(Marwick, 2015, p. 139)*

Micro-celebrities for massive micro-environments and the massive popularity of ordinary people are two of the poles that make visible the forms of use of the personal image as a vehicle of *popularity*, *fame*, and *recognition*.

In the context of what Marwick has called an economy of attention, *attracting attention* has been developed on a planetary scale in conjunction with the impulse to live an experience in and through the image of a set of practices around enjoyment and gratifications.

There is a particular mode of enjoyment associated with social networks in general and Instagram in particular: *instagramtification*.[1]

The arrangement of connections according to *followers* (similar to other networks), the likes in the shape of a heart, the profile descriptions, and the modalities of the most recent *status* on Instagram prepare and predispose people for the game of rewards.

In Instagram in particular, the images must trigger, awaken, and/or provoke expressions of like-dislike, attraction-repulsion, and empathy-indifference; what it cannot fail to produce is the satisfaction in the immediate enjoyment of making images that impact and produce emotions. Image makers have a great time capturing experiences.

Gratus comes from Latin grātus, from Indo-European *gʷerH- ("to welcome, welcome, praise"). Compare Sanskrit गृणाति (gṛṇā́ti, "to praise") (Wiktionary, 2022); in some sense being followed, praised, and congratulated for the ability to attract attention and produce a sensation is one of the secrets of Instagram.

This action of enjoyment consists of pleasant experiences associated with the photos/images; they are connected with micro-compensations and produced in the product that is to be produced. Eating, drinking, losing weight, and being with friends are pleasant when transformed into images. Nice to see each other and to be seen in a pleasant *situation*. The type of ice cream that I deserved, what I waited so long for, what deserves to be put in public, the object of the house that I wanted, etc. Small *paid* compensations are inscribed in the images and their experience.

According to the analysis that we have been carrying out and to dialogue from one of the possible reflection edges, with the challenge of knowing/living/looking while playing, in the next sections we will deal with outlining some preliminary ideas.

One of the fields of inquiry and uses of Instagram is that of politics, as argued by Pineda et al. (2020):

> Social networks have been linked to phenomena such as the personalization of politics (…) and at the same time they are a tool useful for creating political propaganda dedicated to politainment and the creation of celebrities (…) Considering the voter's ability to participate on these platforms, social networks become important when it comes to showing oneself to the electorate in a close way, establishing a connection emotional. In this context, the celebration of the candidate and the star politicians are linked to their consideration as individuals (…) and, consequently, to personalization. Personalization has become an element related to the de-ideologization of politics in the field of infotainment programs (…), and is present in politics mediated in social networks.
>
> *(Pineda et al., 2020, p. 83)*

You can also find works on discipline and control through the management of bodies/emotions through Instagram, as is the case in the work by Leitzke and Rigo where they conclude the following:

> As pointed out in the analysis of this work, statements circulate on Instagram linked to practices of confession, intervention and manipulation of the body, between body, health and beauty, own translation health maintenance strategies and normalization of subjects, prescription, accountability

> and creation of desires. On the platform, individuals seek to control each other and themselves, the power relations, but also control and surveillance strategies.
>
> *(Leitzke & Rigo, 2020, p. 9)*

Instagram also participates in the general characteristics of the virtual/mobile/digital world regarding the phenomena of modification of self-esteem and comparison:

This growth at an exponential pace suggests that online social networks play a relevant role in the way individuals interact and present themselves to one another nowadays (Kross et al., 2013).

> This form of interaction and presentation to the world can impact on the formation of self-concept or even the capability of individuals to assess their self-concepts (their self-esteem). Recent studies point to the effects, positive and negative, of the use of Instagram on self-assessment and, also, on interpersonal relationships, which are an important pillar of self-esteem.
>
> *(Seabra Fagundes et al., 2020, p. 712)*

As a study from Latin America shows diverse and complex relationships between users and celebrities are also made effective, where fashion and intensity differ from reflection and communication.

> The activity between the influencers and their audiences presents some variations in Peru and Colombia; Although in the first country the influencers accumulate millions of user participations, in Colombia the rates rise, mainly in those that position themselves as leaders. Although a fact that is repeated in both groups is the decrease in the emission of text written by the public, an action that demonstrates an audience with a tendency to immediacy and that, although they like content, they do not spend more time to give an opinion on it.
>
> *(Gonzalez-Carrion & Aguaded, 2020, p. 171)*

In the context of fashion bloggers in Romania:

> Following a marketing perspective, Instagram fashion bloggers act as opinion leaders who exert their influence by providing a form of interaction that the professional fashion world lacks, while also representing sources of inspiration for their followers. On Instagram, the most popular users who are able to exert a major influence over other users are called "influencers". In terms of digital communication strategies, the power of word-of-mouth should not be underestimated as it is seen by some as more effective than any other form of planned message. Indeed, in a digitalized world,

> a review or a personal endorsement is still more valued than a company's press releases and customer service, which means that personal fashion blogs hold a strong advantage. Furthermore, as Marwick points out, there are many benefits that come with being a fashion blogger: from invitations to fashion shows, to free clothes and brand collaborations; encouraging more women, since females are predominantly the ones running fashion blogs, to start their own blog (2013, p. 1). Success of a fashion blogger can also lead to collaborations and sponsorships of brands, but, even then, they will be expected to continue posting from an "authentic" perspective by their followers (Marwick, 2013, p. 4).
>
> *(Lungeanu & Parisi, 2018, p. 29)*

In another sense, Instagram has been explored to investigate the difficult contemporary connections between health and youth. In this regard Carceller-Maicas (2015) concludes:

> The more diverse, broad and enriching our communicative relationship with our young informants, the greater the quantity and quality of information that they will share with us, and therefore the greater the data that we will have to carry out our research. When talking about youth health, and more specifically the phenomenon of self-management of emotional discomfort, there are many information gaps that can be found. Creating a good link, with a dialogical relationship based on horizontality and reciprocity between researcher and researched, becomes key to being able to fill the aforementioned gaps. And it is at this point that using a new generation dialogic communication tool like Instagram can help. We have to get to know our informants, get closer to their world and adapt to their usual ways of communicating to make it as easy as possible for them to express their experiences and emotional anguish.
>
> *(Carceller-Maicas, 2015, p. 233)*

In the conclusion of their Thesis "Virtual Ethnographic Experiences from Instagram – Practices of Staging Identities through Food Photos", Brandhøj and Neergaard Jørgensen (2013) argue the following:

> By conducting this qualitative pilot-study using virtual ethnographic methods, focusing on online data gathering alone, the researchers found this methodology applicable to the aim of capturing staging of identities through shared photos of food on Instagram. The researchers have succeeded in capturing everyday practices of the users, within the scope of qualitative research validity. the data gathered is to be considered as snapshots of everyday online practices, of the researched users' lived lives on the specific days of communicating with the researchers and other Instagram users.
>
> *(Brandhøj & Neergaard Jørgensen, 2013, p. 50)*

## 2.2 Instagram and Soup Kitchens

The methodological strategy consisted of developing a digital ethnography of the collective food assistance practices based on Instagram, making it possible to investigate methodologies that allow us to approach the new phenomena by using technologies as phenomena installed in everyday life. In doing this we can review the binary divisions between "the virtual/the real" and "the online/the offline" in understanding social experiences.

Digital and/or virtual ethnography can be defined in various ways, among others, as shown by Mosquera:

> Cyberspace and cyberculture make adoption necessary of Cyber-anthropology and with it the birth of Ethnography of the cyberculture in new ethnographies called Cybernetnography... Ethnography of Cyberspace... Virtual Ethnography... Anthropology of Media... Mediated Ethnography... Ethnography from/in/through the Internet... all of them as a diversity of names for what in this work is called digital ethnography, but that in Internet studios is better known as "virtual ethnography".
>
> *(Mosquera, 2008, p. 541)*

In another vein, Jörgen Skågeby argues that the online ethnographic process consists of cultural immersion, data collection, and analysis. At the same time, the author points out that reliable interpretations and ethically sound research must be ensured and that members of the studied environment can provide feedback on the research (Skågeby, 2010). Sarah Pink and her colleagues, in the introduction to her book *Digital Ethnography: Principles and Practice*, maintains that in a digital, material, and sensorial scenario, it is necessary to explore the impact of the presence of digital media in the configuration of the techniques and processes through which we practice ethnography (Pink et al., 2016).

For us, the process of digital ethnography can be understood as consisting of four dialectical activities: 1. progressive approach, 2. systematic recording, 3. systematization, and 4. analysis/interpretation.

1. The progressive approach can be understood as a process for which, in the first instance, it is necessary to visualize/navigate the possibilities of the space/field of observation; then, the network or immersion surface is selected according to the problem studied, and finally, the actors and agents involved with the research problem are identified.
2. On the other hand, systematic registration implies the use of record resources (tables, digital instruments), the elaboration of records according to the dimensions/variables of the research, and the design and execution of different record surfaces.
3. The systematization involves a tensional game between classification, organization, and articulation/connection between the observations and

experiences of the subjects involved. From here, they visualize and connect the objects, narrations, and interactions that make up the world of digital life.

4. The analysis/interpretation game should be approached from the dialectic between recursion, continuous immersion, and native-hermeneutic.

As we have argued in the previous chapter, our perspective on bodies, emotions, and collective actions (Scribano, 2017, 2021) can be stated very briefly as follows:

Emotions are therefore practices that transform the world and, based on a biography of sensations, challenge the person, producing recognition of bodily and affective states that involve them in all the modalities of their geometry. Emotions are affective cognitive tendencies that: a) imply a movement, an activity, and a modification of time/space, b) serve as maps to recognize the interaction situations, and c) allow the management of the effects of said interactions. Consequently, the politics of bodies (i.e., the strategies that society accepts to offer a response to the social availability of individuals) is a chapter – and not the least essential – in the instruction manual of power. These strategies are tied and "strengthened" by the politics of emotions that tend to regulate the construction of social sensibility. Politics of emotions require regulating and making bearable the conditions under which social order is produced and reproduced. In this context, we understand that social bearability mechanisms are structured around a set of practices that have become embodied and that are oriented towards a systematic avoidance of social conflict.

As we have explained in Chapter 1, *practices of wanting*, *feeling practices*, and *interstitial practices* are three concepts that become relevant in the context of interstitial practices. Associations between the aforementioned practices, social bearability mechanisms, and devices to regulate sensations might allow us to understand the state of social sensibilities better.

It is in this framework that the recognition and critical analysis of the emotional ecologies that we have at hand acquire importance, which can in some way help to relocate the pieces of the game, which will be beyond whether we accept their presence or not. An emotional ecology can be characterized by three factors: first, in each politics of sensibilities, a set of emotions are constituted connected by aspects of family, the kinship of practices, proximity, and emotional amplitudes. Second, this set of emotions constitutes a reference system for each of these emotions in a particular geopolitical and geocultural context that gives them a specific valence. Third, they are groups of feeling practices whose particular experience regarding an element of life can only be understood in its collective context.

From this context, it can be inferred that the modes of expression rooted in and based on the sensibilities of the subjects are tied to historical practices that seek a heterodox place for domination and should be read as a task of rehumanizing relations between humans and as politics. It is obvious that the expressive resources are anchored in criteria and aesthetic valuations of materials, production, and artistic sense, and that these are in turn dependent on a particular historical context. However, for the expressive resources of collective actions and social protests, there is a making visible and perceptible that was previously invisible and inaudible.

Within the framework of what has been developed so far, in the following section we show some of the results of the digital ethnography carried out and which gave rise to this chapter.

## 2.3 "Logos" and Photos: Expressive Resources of the Approaching

Instagram allows the researcher to select as a specific example of inquiry the online interview, the online survey, the analysis of photos and videos – to have a semiotic approach or to choose various possibilities of discourse analysis.

In the context of the Covid-19 pandemic, in the world in general but Latin America in particular, there was a food supply crisis, which in turn led to the appearance of thousands of humanitarian groups that organized to help people who could not guarantee their daily food supply.

In this framework, we carry out through Instagram the inquiry that we now summarize.

One of the features of the record made in our digital ethnography was to highlight the images used as "logos" of identity, the photos associated with these images, the names of the groups, and the comments or "posts" made around them: in this section, we will make a synthesis of the first analysis of some a) logos or identification images, and b) photos and text images. The digital ethnography was carried out during July and August 2020, months in which in almost all countries that were included in our analysis there were strong restrictions on movement and prolonged confinement.

The methodological strategy consisted of developing a digital ethnography of the collective practices of food assistance during the Covid-19 pandemic based on activity on Instagram. This ethnography involves three basic components: a) the identification of at least one collective experience per Latin American country as a *qualitative sampling by exemplarity*. This type of sampling is selected when the phenomena to be studied can be understood through the observation of exemplary experiences that contain a paradigmatic configuration of what is being observed (Scribano, 2008), b) analysis of 17 countries and 24 dimensions of the collective practices, and c) the conduct of interviews with the organizers through Instagram.

These observations were useful to reconstruct the particularities and differences in each one of the components of the #Feed, Stories, and Chats and the news of the social networks of the groups investigated. The dimensions observed and recorded were: name of organization; name on Instagram; link; country; resource used; logo; message emphasized; image/video used as identification; colours used; source of donations; stocks of political, institutional, or state linkages; existence of predominant gender; presence of children; age of organizers; opening or closing to participation; diet; how they see themselves; how they understand the context; which emotions prevail; what text they use to identify themselves; what hashtags they used; who speaks to them; who "likes" their activities; and other observations.

The process was carried out taking into account the names of the groups or organizations as an indication of the activity they carried out in connection with the context of the country where they were located.

### *1. Name*

1. Olla Popular Paraguay
2. Olla Comunitaria Bolivia
3. Olla Popular Nuevo Encuentro
4. Olla común solidaria Estación Central
5. Alimenta Venezuela
6. Olla Popular Brazo Oriental
7. Come Honduras
8. Avanzando Juntos Guatemala
9. Ejército de Salvación México
10. ONG Guaguacuna
11. Comedores Sociales Puerto Rico
12. Ayudemos Panamá
13. Olla común
14. Lxs Nadie Bogotanos
15. Ayudanos a Ayudar
16. Nutriendo con el corazón
17. Mano Solidaria El Salvador
18. Projeto Solidario Abracando a comunidade
19. Asociación Pato Amarillo

### *2. Countries*

1. Paraguay
2. Bolivia
3. Argentina
4. Chile
5. Venezuela
6. Uruguay
7. Honduras
8. Guatemala
9. Mexico
10. Ecuador
11. Puerto Rico

12. Panama
13. Peru
14. Colombia
15. Costa Rica
16. Salvador
17. Brazil

## 2.4 Interview Interpretation

Instagram is a means to show oneself, to buy and sell, to feel through what others feel when they publish their photos or videos, and also to engage politically and socially. This section summarizes some features of how social research can witness that.

In our strategy, we also included a set of online interviews, one for each country, that had the following characteristics: most were asynchronous, people answered very synthetically, and everyone appreciated the concern.

The interviews were very simple – they consisted of three questions, and the answer could be given in writing or orally. Why are you doing this collaboration with people or with soup kitchens? How do you feel about your contribution right now? How are you doing? They were also asked to provide: their age, sex/gender, studies, and place where they lived. Below is an example of the responses.

Responses of male, 27 years old, Montevideo, Uruguay

1. Need and scarcity of policies, without work, without income, difficult to access a plate of food, we noticed, many people, would need help, "we got down to work". Sensation of absence need, impossibility, help, bodily practice.
2. Before we "noticed", then we felt, noticing another experience street situation, eating, sheltering, serving... there are realities of all kinds. Empathy and diagnosis of sensibility.
3. Privileged position by having work and food... the minimum is a privilege..., as a tired group, the government does nothing.

One of the first characteristics we noticed from the interviews is that regarding diagnosis, many say that there are people, compatriots, neighbours from the neighbourhood who are alone. This is how the logic of approximation appears, the logic of empathizing with the other. If he is alone, he cannot be alone because he is nearby. In and through this logic, a practice of feeling is being drawn that implies, for all the organizations and actions against hunger, an axis of their politics of sensibility: an axis of what is structuring the day-to-day, with the imperative of "I cannot leave the other alone" – we are not all alone in the impotence of being without nutrients, of being without food, and of not being able to eat.

A second characteristic of the interviews is the feeling of obligation, of having to do it. It is not about calculation or speculation, it is an opposition to the political economy of morality that only speaks about the individual and self-centredness. Each one of the interviewees mentions, in their own way, the obligation to do something for the other's right, and there is a very important axis of politics ofsensibilities. The subjects that work in these collective practices feel that they are obliged, and then the paradox of meaning is outlined regarding the discovery of the autonomy of being able to decide to do something for others but forced from a political or ethical position. In each of the interviews, questioning appears as the motivation for doing.

A third characteristic, without a doubt, is that everyone says "well… we do this because it also makes us feel good, because it is part of being able to do something, which makes us feel noble, which gratifies us by doing good for others". In this configuration of gratifying yourself by doing good for the other, the paradox is rebuilt with the political economy of morality that points in the direction of immediate enjoyment through self-centred consumption. In this sense, these same practices deny that individualism is the only way to respond to how it is possible to live in capitalism. The gratification paradox does not nullify the challenge of the experience of "co-feeling good" with those who receive, without believing in the moral superiority of the giver.

The fourth common characteristic is to experience, through receiving donations, that they not only have the idea of helping the other but that they also do not feel alone, just as they do not want others to be alone in their absence of food. They also perceive that what they do is a matter of the greater collective – not only those who make the food or distribute the food but a greater, common whole. It is through this experience that "helping" is transformed into a particular feeling of being accompanied by a wider group, which again refers to the identity of the neighbourhood, the city, the homeland, and also refers to the identity of those who are not alone because they go out in search of others.

## 2.5 Knowing Touching: Instapraxis and Touch

A society to see, listen, touch with exposed bodies/emotions, with speakers and viewpoints, are in the first instance what the grammar of Instagram offers us. Instagram has become a social network that hosts a set of social practices that testify to some of the most interesting features of the production, use, and reproduction of images today. Instagram is a social network that allows its users to take and share photos and videos, apply a digital filter to them, and share them on a variety of social networking services such as Facebook, Twitter, Tumblr, and Flickr. The 21st century has been born as a time and space where a redefinition of the policies of the senses in and through Society 4.0, which encompasses the Fourth Industrial Revolution and Instagram, is an excellent example of some of its boundaries.

The second assessment of society today is that, through Instagram, we can perceive the importance of taste, commensality, and food as an experience that has been going on since the construction of "global neighbourhoods" in the main cities of the world, where you can experience food of many different cultures. In a "gourmet" way, something extraordinary is experienced through the modalities of being with others around food, where the particular as well as the exotic takes place.

People photograph themselves and "take a selfie" at the most diverse occasions, from mothers giving birth, through to participants taking part in high-risk activities, to after-sex selfies. It seems that human beings want to show themselves, and Instagram is one of the favourite vehicles to do so. In this context, it must be borne in mind that "'selfie' – a self-portrait made in a reflective object or from arm's length – was selected as word of the year by the Oxford English Dictionary in 2013, and news items about selfies are in the mainstream media daily" (Tiidenberg & Gomez Cruz, 2015, p. 78).

Instagram is used to investigate different types of phenomena, along with which the following can be mentioned: nostalgia (Schiemer & Carlsen, 2016); seduction (Lasén & García, 2015); marketing (Nummmila, 2015); youth health (Carceller-Maicas, 2015); selfies (Souza et al., 2015); consumer behaviour (McCune, 2011); cities (Boy & Uitermark, 2015, 2016); identities in social networks (Lindahl & Öhlund, 2013); and funerals (Gibbs et al., 2015).

Instagram constitutes one of the fundamental steps in current changes in the "visual literacy" of a planet that wants to see everything and instantly:

> What is visual literacy? Human beings interact with the world and interpret it primarily through their eyes. We use our sight to classify individuals into age, gender, racial and ethnic categories. We live in the era of Facebook, Google, Twitter, Instagram gram and other social media, which have radically changed how we communicate, acquire, conceptualize and store information. Smartphones, with built-in cameras, have enabled millennials (individuals born after 1982) to develop forms of visual literacy. The visual is primary.
>
> *(Winddance Twine, 2016, p. 968)*

The "networks" are conductive channels of some modalities of understanding the way of seeing and have become massive on a planetary scale. Instagram does not only socialize images, it shares experiences, practices of feeling, and politics of sensibilities, and through them a way of knowing and making the world.

> The Instagram picture allows the person to experience the feelings of being in the location through a combination of observing the picture with the personally embedded textual and location data within the picture. The comments attached to the picture become the "vox populi" of the overall impression of the experience. This combination of all of the mediated content represents the digital contextualization of the experience.
>
> *(Tilton, 2014, p. 4)*

The kind of images that are commonly encountered on Instagram present a challenge to the criteria of truth, not only about the social world and the "natural" world but especially about the "inner planet" (*sensu* Melucci).

> Millions of adolescents – they use the phone as a mirror. Who is the most beautiful? They ask the little mirror seen by thousands of eyes. And Instagram returns their response: no likes, 315 likes, 17,000 likes. Some numbers to build self-love, a love of one's own image, if there is something of one's own in an image that is built in the image and likeness of the hundreds of thousands of images that the adolescent has seen of other adolescents: they dress just like her, that they wear a similar haircut, similar clothes and that they pose in the places that she frequents or would like to frequent.
>
> *(Potel, 2013, p. 118)*

Daily life becomes extraordinary in and through images. Just as geographers, naturalists, and travellers portrayed the world in times of colonization of the planet, today social networks, and especially Instagram, map the world for us in an instant. Customs, identities, sexualities, sociabilities, experiences, and sensibilities are discovered, produced, distributed, and reproduced from the palm and with the fingertips.

Instagram, as a social practice, fulfils at least three functions that it shares with other social networks: it communicates, distributes/spreads, and produces practices of feeling. It is not necessary to be at an event to know what happened, who "attended", and what it felt like: Instagram (like any social network) makes it live for us. Own photos, snapshots, re-sent photos, from albums (own and others), produced, arranged, spontaneous, and retouched, are some of the multiple possibilities that always having a "camera at hand" enables.

However, Instagram has the particularity of focusing its actions on the image, and with this, it explores/exploits what can be referred to as ICI: immersion, connectivity, and intensity. The image not only immerses us in the landscape but also in its experience, making it possible to merge with the transmitted sensation: it is a producer of sensations and triggers emotions. The image re-unites, binds, facilitates, and prolongs understanding, allowing and facilitating being in contact. The image summarizes, synthesizes, enhances, reproduces, and impacts; it always implies a reaction.

Taking Instagram as a registration surface and at the same time as a stage where social practices are carried out, we have at least two interaction spaces – one associated with practices outside the network and the other referred to as the "inside" of the network. The former reflects the state of affairs of the social structuring processes, the latter the one that arises from the network and has an impact outside of it.

Instagram is an inscription surface where millions upon millions of photographed experiences and the results of image makers take shape: one way to systematize them is through a typology of said images.

Hu, Manikonda, and Kambhampati (2014) showed that it is possible to initially identify an approximation of a typology of images that can be found on Instagram: friends, food, devices/artefacts, photo messages, pets, "activities", selfies, and fashion. This classification enables us to think of Instagram as a storage device for experiences around what becomes the object of the gaze and the subject of the expressive speech act at the moment of being captured. The discontinuous journey between the photo, the object, the capture, the "capturer", the image, and the recipient makes this particular social network the paradigmatic example of networks. Capturing not photographing, experience not object, for me not for the other, are the co-edges of a sinuous frontier between sharing and consuming.

We are living in a stage of humanity where our senses converge with the world of technology in search of "aids/orthopaedics" to say what is and how we experience reality. Instagram is a paradigmatic example and a metonymic effect of the practices that are changing our ways of producing sociabilities, experiences, and sensibilities.

Telephones, heaters, air conditioners, car locks, refrigerators, televisions, computers, and tablets, all are or can be, at present, digital objects.

At www.macstories.net, managed by Federico Vittici, you can read about the already old iPhone 7 and its haptic system:

> Haptic feedback provides a tactile response, like a touch, that attracts attention and reinforces both actions and the events. While many system-supplied interface elements (for example, selectors, switches, and controllers) automatically provide haptic feedback, you can use feedback generators to add your own feedback to custom views and controls.
>
> *(Mac, 2016)*

The instaimage was born in a context of technological and productive upheavals, institutional slides, and a resurgence of the importance of the hand as an organ connected to thought.

Seeing-feeling begins with touching-looking at oneself. The image (today more than ever?) is an intersubjective production that acquires the characteristic of an instantiated practice at the moment that the capture of the production made for the viewer takes place. While I make an image, I touch the surface of a device that I need to look at to see myself feeling what I want to know and make known.

Today, seeing is touching and feeling what is seen. The fingertips make contact with the screen(s), the glass receives the pressure of decision-making, and sliding navigates the menu of options that the previous selection enabled. When we see a photo we are touching it, at times almost imperceptibly, but most of the time with that moment of monitoring that prevents inaccuracies: unwanted likes, improper uploads, and incorrect stalking.

The production of the instaimage is guided by capturing not photographing, seeking a capture, not a photo, trying to transmit an experience, not an object, in a massive and radically self-produced way; it is a synthesis (perhaps the "willow" filter)[2] of a scopic regimen that since ancient times produces "new" consequences. Although every image seeks to convey experiences, the instaimage is based on this quality of "portraying" and uses it as a starting point.

Are the modifications in our scopic regime some modifications in our value system? If an ethic corresponds to every aesthetic transformation and to a policy, perhaps the answer is yes.

## 2.6 Instagram and Social Research

In line with the intentions of this chapter and the general spirit of this book, it is interesting to understand how Instagram is an application that is part of the virtual/mobile/digital world and constitutes a component of the so-called digital methods. Barbosa Prado and Zago conceptualize digital methods as follows:

> Digital methods, in short, concern the development of new epistemological, methodological and research-oriented perspectives social with the web. The purpose of digital methods, for Rogers (2014), is to reorient the domain of research on the internet, by studying and redefining what he calls the methods of the medium, as they evolve, namely: methods incorporated into online devices that cover techniques for collecting, classifying and analyzing natively digital data (such as tags, hyperlinks, etc.), aiming at the production of cultural and social.
>
> *(Barbosa Prado & Zago, 2018, p. 44)*

Instagram produces native digital data with the speciality that it is an excellent vehicle to concretize the dissemination of content produced with the tools that the app itself contains (filters for example); storage, circulation, and reproduction of materials from other networks and development of a particular interaction environment.

Instagram is part of the digital methods because it allows the identification, systematization, and analysis of information according to the specific ways of its functions, for example, the stories and the assignment of the relevance of the same.

As can be seen in this chapter, Instagram is a central contribution when it comes to the redefinition of social research in the current era, given its ability to capture the modifications of emotional ecologies at the same time that the social action is carried out.

Instagram also has the advantage of being able to capture and manage images where the identification and collection of users' data is possible, including sharing this information with the institutions with which it interacts and the companies it is connected to, etc. Regarding data management by social networks, Silva Assumpção and his colleagues argue the following:

> The ease with which images are now captured and shared across networks social media such as Facebook and Instagram contributes to the empowerment of corporations managing these networks. An example of this empowerment is that, together, Facebook and Instagram, may constitute one of the largest databases of images of the world, mainly because they have data such as "who", "when", "where" and "what" added to these images – data collected through facial recognition, metadata, location data and tags.
>
> *(Silva Assumpção, 2015, p. 44)*

It is on this basis that Instagram (and the rest of the networks) and the "dispute" over metadata will almost certainly be one of the components of the theoretical/political/epistemological discussion of the use of such applications as instruments of inquiry.

Santos David and his colleagues (2019) introduce a very interesting aspect by critically analyzing Instagram as a teaching method for middle schools, where research support is one of the possibilities identified. In a similar sense, Costa in his work on the use of Instagram as a teaching and dissemination tool in university education maintains that:

> In times of technology and information sharing, social media play an important role in the dissemination of works by Brazilian universities. Instagram, a social media for sharing images and videos, can be used as tool for scientific dissemination, reaching an audience that seeks this type of information. The Laboratory of Microscopy of the Federal University of Santa Catarina – Campus Araranguá created a profile of the biological area with the username atlasmicroscopia that has as purpose the sharing of images taken in the laboratory coming from practical classes of the courses of the health area.
>
> *(Costa, 2019, p. 1)*

In another sense, this book seeks to draw attention to the connections between digital research and creativity. Formiga Sobrinho and his colleagues (2014) in their article "Creativity on Instagram as an innovation tool for organizations" present how creativity and the Internet have become a central axis through which companies and institutions communicate, inquire, and innovate.

Researching, investigating, creating, and innovating are practices that Instagram makes possible and that the social sciences cannot stop recreating to use for social research.

Images, audio, texts, and videos populate the virtual/mobile/digital world and are presented as the components of the development of research at this time. The articulation in an unanchored time/space, in an instantaneous topology of action, and the wide possibilities of participation in the elaboration of information, make Instagram a basic application to create social research environments.

Within the framework of all the above, it is possible to return to some axes that connect directly with the objective of the book.

Firstly, we have shown that Instagram is a more than adequate vehicle to capture sensibilities as understood by synthesized empirical research.

Secondly, some of the features by which Instagram allows the articulation of various components of social research have been outlined, showing how Instagram is becoming an effective and efficient tool.

Thirdly, what it means to know and see touching has been summarized, something we have maintained for a long time (Scribano, 2021), and as one of the central features of Society 4.0, this has a central importance for the ways of generating knowledge in the future.

## Notes

1 The term Instagramtification is proposed by Oloo (2013), but here it is used differently.
2 A type of filter for photos on Instagram that creates a monochrome, old-fashioned, dreamy impression.

## References

Barbosa Prado, J. A., & Zago, G. da S. (2018). Ecologia dos aplicativos de mídias sociais da Google Play Store sob a ótica dos métodos digitais e da análise de redes para mídias sociais. *Galáxia, 38*, 40–55. https://doi.org/10.1590/1982-2554232726

Boy, J. D., & Uitermark, J. (2015). Capture and share the city: Mapping Instagram's uneven geography. In Conference. Amsterdam Paper: RC21 International Conference on the Ideal City: Between Myth and Reality. Representations, Policies, Contradictions and Challenges for Tomorrow's Urban Life. Urbino, Italy, August. http://www.rc21.org/en/conferences/urbino2015/

Boy, J. D., & Uitermak, J. (2016). How to study the city on instagram. *PLoS ONE 11*(6), e0158161. https://doi.org/10.1371/journal.pone.0158161

Brandhøj, M., & Neergaard Jørgensen, L (2013). *Virtual Ethnographic Experiences from Instagram: Practices of Staging Identities through Food Photos*. Aalborg University.

Carceller-Maicas, N. (2015). Jóvenes, Salud y Redes Sociales. Instagram como herramienta de investigación en la comunicación de la salud. *MÈTODE Science Studies Journal, 88*, 80–87. https://doi.org/10.7203/metode.6.6555

Costa, F. V. (2019). Uso do Instagram como ferramenta de estudo: análise de um perfil da área biológica. *Research, Society and Development, 8*(10), e238101360. https://doi.org/10.33448/rsd-v8i10.1360

Formiga Sobrinho, A. B., & Mota Barbosa, A. (2014). Criatividade no instagram como ferramenta de inovação para as organizações. *Signos do Consumo, 6*(1), 125–137.

Gibbs, M., Meese, J., Arnold, M., Nansen, B., & Carter, M. (2015). Funeral and instagram: death, social media, and platform vernacular. *Information, Communication & Society, 18*(3), 255–268. https://doi.org/10.1080/1369118X.2014.987152.

Gonzalez-Carrion, E. L., & Aguaded, I. (2020). Interaction processes in Latin American Instagramers. The case of Peru and Colombia during 2019. *Revista de Comunicación, 19*(2), 161–174.

Hu, Y., Manikonda, L., & Kambhampati, S. (2014). What we instagram: A first analysis of instagram photo content and user types. In Conference. International AAAI

Conference on Web and Social Media, North America. Retrieved from https://www.aaai.org/ocs/index.php/ICWSM/ICWSM14/paper/view/8118

Lasén, A., & García, A. (2015). '. . . but I haven't got a body to show': Self-pornification and male mixed feelings in digitally mediated seduction practices. *Sexualities*, *18*(5/6), 714–730.

Leitzke, A. T. da S., & Rigo, L. C. (2020). Sociedade de controle e redes sociais na internet: #saúde e #corpo no instagram. *Movimento*, *26*, e26062. https://doi.org/10.22456/1982-8918.100688

Lindahl, G., & Öhlund, M. (2013). *Personal Branding Through Imagification in Social Media: Identity Creation and Alteration Through Images*. Master Thesis of Science in Business and Economics, Stockholm University. Retrieved from https://www.diva-portal.org/smash/record.jsf?pid=diva2%3A685990&dswid=9588

Lungeanu, M. I., & Parisi, L. (2018). What makes a fashion blogger on Instagram? The Romanian case study. *Observatorio (OBS*) Journal*, *1*(1), 28–53.

Mac. (2016). *Mac Stories*. Retrieved from www.macstories.net/

Marwick, A. (2015). Instafame: Luxury selfies in the attention economy. *Public Culture*, *27*(1), 137–160.

McCune, Z. (2011). *Consumer Production in Social Media Networks: A Case Study of the "Instagram" iPhone App*. Dissertation. Phil in Modern Society & Global Transformation at the University of Cambridge. Supervisor: Dr. John Thompson. Submitted 9 June.

Mosquera, M. A. (2008). De la Etnografía antropológica a la Etnografía virtual. *Fermentum*, *18*(53), 532–549.

Nummmila, M. (2015). *Successful social media marketing on Instagram. Case: @minoshoes*. Bachelor's. Thesis. Degree Programme in IB. Haaga-Helia, University of Applied Sciencc.

Oloo, F. L. (2013). *"Instagratification": Uses and Gratification of Instagram. by University Students for Interpersonal Communication*. Thesis. Submitted to the Institute of Graduate Studies and Research in partial fulfilment of the requirements for the Degree of Master of Arts in Communication and Media Studies Eastern Mediterranean University July 2013 Gazimağusa, North Cyprus.

Pineda, A., Barragán-Romero, A. I., & Bellido-Pérez, E. (2020). Representación de los principales líderes políticos y uso propagandístico de Instagram en España. *Cuadernos.info*, *47*, 80–110. https://doi.org/10.7764/cdi.47.1744

Pink, S., Horst, H., Postill, J., Hjorth, L., Lewis, T., & Tacchi, J. (2016). Introduction. In *Digital Ethnography: Principles and Practice*. Sage.

Potel, H. (2013). Instante programado. Instagram, texto instantáneo, repetición y acontecimiento. *Arte en las redes sociales*, *2013*, 117–126.

Santos David, F. de F., Borges, A., da Silva, A., Baldasso, G., Souza Marculino, C. H., Almeida, J. V., & Bueno Soltau, S. (2019). Uma proposta de uso do Instagram em metodologia aplicável em disciplinas do Ensino Médio. *Research, Society and Development*, *8*(4), e1684959. https://doi.org/10.33448/rsd-v8i4.959

Schiemer, B., & Carlsen, H. B. (2016). Nostalgia, irony and collectivity in late-modern culture: The ritual watching of The Disney Christmas Show in Scandinavia. *Acta Sociológica*, *60*(2), 158–175.

Scribano, A. (2008). *El Proceso de Investigación Social Cualitativo*. Prometeo.

Scribano, A. (2017). *Normalization, Enjoyment and Bodies/emotions: Argentine Sensibilities*. Nova Science Publishers.

Scribano, A. (2021). *Colonization of Inner Planet. 21st Century Social Theory from the Politics of Sensibilities*. Routledge.

Seabra Fagundes, L., Azevedo Marot, T., & Natividade, JC. (2020). Use of instagram, social comparison, and personality as predictors of self-esteem. *Psico-USF, Bragança Paulista*, *25*(4), 711–724. https://doi.org/10.1590/1413/82712020250410

Senft, T. M. (2008). *Camgirls: Celebrity and Community in the Age of Social Networks* (Vol. 4). Peter Lang Publishing.

Silva Assumpção, F., Gonçalves Santana, R. C., da Costa Santos, V.A., & Leopoldina P. (2015). Coleta de dados a partir de imagens: considerações sobre a privacidade dos usuários em redes sociais. *Em Questão*, *21*(2), 31–4.

Skågeby, J. (2010). Online ethnographic methods: Towards a qualitative understanding of virtual community practices. In D. Ben Kei (ed.), *Handbook of Research on Methods and Techniques for Studying Virtual Communities: Paradigms and Phenomena* (pp. 410–428). IGI Global.

Souza, F., De Las Casas, D., Flores V., Youn, S., Cha, M., Quercia, D., & Almeida, V. (2015). Dawn of the selfie era: The whos, wheres, and hows of selfies on Instagram. In Proceedings of the 2015 ACM on Conference on Online Social Networks. Palo Alto, CA: ACM, 221–231. https://doi.org/10.1145/2817946.2817948

Tiidenberg, K., & Gomez Cruz, E. (2015). Selfies, image and the re-making of the body. *Body & Society*, *21*(4), 77–102.

Tilton, S. (2014). Mobile public memory: The (digital/ physical) (artifacts/souvenirs) of the (archiver/tourist). *SAGE Open*, 1–9.

Turner, G. (2004). *Understanding Celebrity*. Sage.

Wiktionary. (2022). Gratus. Retrieved from https://en.wiktionary.org/wiki/pleasant

Winddance Twine, F. (2016). Visual sociology in a discipline of words: Racial literacy, visual literacy and qualitative research methods. *Sociology*, *50*(5), 967–974.

# 3

# WHATSAPP, COMMUNICATE, REGISTER, KNOW

## Argentinean Social Conflict and the March of Hondurans to the USA

### Introduction

The main objective of the chapter is to present a research experience using WhatsApp, especially from a methodological/epistemic/theoretical perspective. This motivation is accompanied by the conviction that the social sciences must deepen the evaluation of new forms of inquiry.

In achieving the proposed, the following will be carried out: a) the reader is introduced to the outstanding features of the connections between WhatsApp and social research, b) two experiences of an investigation are described: The Everyday Gaze about social conflict and hunger context, and the caravan of Hondurans who migrated to the USA in 2018, c) some notes on the emotional ecologies found are presented, and d) some consequences and learnings are synthesized.

This chapter is a double opportunity to see, on the one hand, how sensible problems such as conflict and migration can be addressed with digital inquiry devices, and on the other, how the confluence of voice, drawing, photo, instant call, and automatic register make WhatsApp an ideal instrument to design new inquiry devices.

In this context, the experiences narrated in the chapter are presented in such a way that the reader can appreciate how these devices allow capturing, from perception of the sensations to reach the emotions of the people who are the subjects of the inquiry.

### 3.1 WhatsApp: Some Research Examples

As Guiñez-Cabrera and Mansilla-Obando (2021) write, WhatsApp in an educational context is also identified as a space for meeting, collaboration, and creativity.

DOI: 10.4324/9781003319771-4

> In addition, Bouhnik and Deshen (2014) conclude in their study that WhatsApp creates an atmosphere that supports interaction, peer collaboration, and content sharing. Ali (2017) also indicates that this social network, from the perspective of smartphones, allows you to connect with peers and learn collaboratively at any time. Likewise, Gómez and Shafirova (2016), Comas-Quinn, De los Arcos and Mardomingo (2012) and Palacios (2020) confirm that WhatsApp favours collaborative learning, as well as different forms of interaction and social participation, in addition to the fact that establish different roles among the participants of a group (Gómez and Shafirova, 2016).
>
> *(Guiñez-Cabrera & Mansilla-Obando, 2021, p. 60)*

In the preceding quote, you can see the set of quotes that support what this chapter also wants to maintain regarding the impossibility of "distinguishing" the real/virtual in the mobile/digital world.

The connections between memes, popular discourse, and politics that Martínez Rolán and Piñeiro Otero (2017) take up in their article "The use of memes in political conversation 2.0 an approach to an ephemeral mobilization" makes it clear how sending memes through WhatsApp is a vehicle for expression and creativity, an aspect of its use that this chapter wants to underline.

On the other hand, negative results can be observed from the use of WhatsApp that involve already "well-established" violence and inequalities, such as gender-based violence:

> In light of the information collected, we can conclude that the technological medium, today, is a factor of more gender-based violence in young couples. In addition to being the means most used by this population for contact with their peers, it offers a whole set of behaviors protected by the offerings of technology to achieve many of the effects of violence.
>
> *(Romero Oliva et al., 2016, p. 23)*

As can be seen, the uses of WhatsApp have already been extensively examined for various issues and from various theoretical and methodological perspectives.

An example of this multiplicity is the use of the application by children, adolescents, and young people: how for the majority (almost 84% of those surveyed) of a sample of middle school students, WhatsApp is considered essential, interesting, and fun (Fernández & del Barrio Fernández, 2017), how the keys to its success are ease of use, being without cost, universality, mobility, and innovation (Rubio-Romero & Perlado Lamo de Espinosa, 2015), and it has also been observed that the variables of personality and anxiety have great weight in the problematic use of WhatsApp in adolescents (Tresáncoras et al., 2017).

Another field that is very illustrative for this book and chapter is the studies of the connection of WhatsApp with politics: the importance of the use of WhatsApp in dissemination, reception, and claims of the messages of a political campaign that can modify the opinions, perceptions, and sensibilities of citizens (Piaia & Alves, 2020), as an attractive instrument for carrying out social and political protests (Zumárraga-Espinosa, 2021), and also as a contribution to the transformation of dialogue and social conversation as democratization of the technology that has enabled new instruments of connection between citizens and political parties (Losada Díaz & Zamora Medina, 2021).

In the context of the above, it is possible to perceive at least three aspects that the studies carried out using WhatsApp reveal that are key to understanding the uses of WhatsApp in the investigation of sensibilities and emotions: a) WhatsApp is a means of expressing emotions, b) it is a communication channel for perceptions regarding various problems, and c) it is easy and agile to use.

### 3.1.1 Virtualities and Social Inquiry

In just a little over ten years, the interactions between the face-to-face social world, the virtual world, and the "mobile" world of cell phones and tablets have grown exponentially, not only in their size (number of participants and devices) but also in their commodification and commercial value.

The social marketing firm Simply Measured in its 2016 report reports that: "according to the eMarketer Report of April 2016, the expected earnings for social networks will exceed 32.91 billion dollars in 2016, with a growth of 30.9% compared to 2015" (Simply Measured, 2016, p. 2).

This should not be forgotten when assessing which surface of inquiry the experience presented here moves in – to which we must add the material, cognitive-affective resources, and the skills that are created in the border and co-border between virtuality and social networks.

In this direction, in 2013, as a future agenda on possible studies on the virtual world, bodies, and emotions, we argued, among other things, that: the Internet presents a great opportunity to investigate the transformation of bodies and emotions in and through this "ethno-space", that these cyberspaces generated new modalities of instantiating emotions, that in these contexts, the word, the image, and sound are put at the service of the social presentation of the person, social cooperation, modifying perception, sensation, and memory, and that all this made us think of a redefinition of orthopaedic and superfluous bodies that are built in our societies – that when thinking about Everyday Glances was not only as a theoretical background but also as a methodological warning.

In the game world, inquiries were also made with theoretical/methodological intentionality, as pointed out by Williams (2009) in his work on virtual worlds:

> Virtual worlds research is a dynamic interdisciplinary area and growing in the social sciences and humanities. Sociological theory can play an important role in the conceptualization and study of virtual worlds. Drawing on data from ethnographic projects on two different types of virtual worlds, an asynchronous text-based forum on the Internet and a multiplayer online

> game, I consider the social and cultural similarities that these two types of virtual worlds have with each other, despite their radical difference in forms and functions.
>
> From the last decade of the last century, studies on what was happening on the Internet, what was beginning to happen in the virtual world and how this gave rise to new styles and sources of research multiplied: the construction of the " online personalities" (Paap and Raybeck, 2005), on the "architectures" of interaction in the nascent social networks (Papacharissi, 2009) and on the characteristics of the new phenomena that were appearing in the world of globalized communication. (Mollett, Moran and Dunleavy 2011).
>
> *(2009, p. 3)*

As De Sena and Lisdero maintain:

> currently we can identify various processes and tools that are conducted through the Internet: semi-structured interviews (Al-Saggaf & Williamson, 2004), research through blogs (LaBanca, 2011; Chenail, 2011a), virtual ethnography (Domínguez et al., 2007; Hine, 2000) and the use of YouTube (Chenail, 2011b), E-Mail interviews (Muir Houston, 2008; Bampton & Cowton, 2002), by MSM ( Yeslam A l-Saggaf & Kristy Williamson, 2004; Vanessa and Gavin, 2009), online discussion groups (Rezabek, 2000), through the "post" of social networks (Piscitelli, et al., 2010; Goodinds, 2011), lifecasting or videos transmitted online in real time (Montoya and Vásquez, 2011), just to mention a few.
>
> *(2015, p. 4)*

It is also known that for a long time there has been research into, through, and about the digital/mobile in connection with the processes of social structuring and conflictuality: about the impact of Facebook and social networks on union organizations (Bryson et al., 2010), digital work in the redefinitions of the international division of labour (Fuchs, 2016), the advent of the platform economy (Cingolani, 2016), and the internationalization of call centres (Lisdero, 2010).

It becomes more complex if you keep in mind that Society 4.0, among many other things, has transformed the potential of communicating through photographs, videos, and audio expressed with cell phones and smartphones. What also occurs are devices used to record, portray, and interpret the world, as Lansen and Garcia (2015) argue in their study on photography, auto-pornography, and social networks:

> Contemporary practices of digital photography are connecting sociability, embodiment, and subjectivity, especially with the convergence of digital cameras, mobile phones, and social media. (...) The ubiquity of cameras and the increasing display and sharing of images online reveal changes

> in the uses and meanings of everyday photographic practices. Enjoyment and experimentation are common features of camera phones and the use of digital cameras, similarly found in their uses for erotic purposes. These changes are made possible by the ease of digital production and the low cost of production for individuals.
>
> *(Lansen & Garcia, 2015, p. 717)*

These worlds in transformation, these technological possibilities, and the redefinition of the cognitive skills necessary to live a plurality of worlds of life, enhanced by the materiality of each of them, open up a set of challenges for the social sciences.

### 3.1.2 WhatsApp and Social Research

Annie Dayani Ahad and Syamimi Md Ariff Lim (2014) in their presentation on the impact of WhatsApp on the students of the Brunei Darussalam University, at the International Conference on Communication and Media, maintain that:

> Since its introduction in 2009, WhatsApp, a mobile instant messaging application, has reached 500 million users worldwide, sharing 700 million photos and 100 million videos per day (Acton & Koum, 2014). Built as an alternative to short message service (SMS), WhatsApp offers real-time text messaging or communication, including the facility to share information (for example, contact list) or multimedia content (for example, audio, video files, images, and location data).
>
> *(Ahad & Lim, 2014, p. 189)*

It must be added that in recent years, voice and video calls and the encryption of communications via WhatsApp have been added. WhatsApp includes certain qualities and facilities that are very clearly understood when compared to other application networks.

It is important to note that WhatsApp represents for many an application through which close relationships are facilitated and deepened, which makes it a more than adequate vehicle to observe said relationships. O'Hara, Massimi, Harper, Rubens, and Morris maintain the following at the end of their study on the impact of WhatsApp on daily life based on the concept of dwelling (*sensu* Ingold) in terms of inhabiting the intersection of spatiality and temporality:

> In conclusion, our research demonstrates how WhatsApp is used by our participants as a key component of their way of living with others. Placing it this way, we place it within the ebb and flow of lives lived together, within the web of other connections, both real and virtual. Along with these other connections, we argue that it is constitutive of felt life with those with whom we live. This helps draw attention not only to the

**TABLE 3.1** Comparison of Instant Messaging Tools between Social Media Platforms

| | *Email* | *SMS* | *Facebook Groups* | *Twitter* | *WhatsApp* |
|---|---|---|---|---|---|
| **Cost** | Free | Paid | Free | Free | Up to $1 per year |
| **Accessibility** | Ability to change text size | Ability to change text size | Fixed text size | Fixed text size | Ability to change text size |
| **Create a group** | Possible | Possible | Easy | Not characteristic of the app | Easy |
| **Add and remove members of a group** | Not possible | Possible | Requires participant approval | Requires participant approval | Easy |
| **Having a smooth conversation in a group** | Not natural | Not possible | Easy | Not characteristic of the app | Easy |
| **Privacy** | Relatively high | Relatively high | Relatively low | Relatively low | Relatively high |
| **Collaborative learning** | Characteristic of the app | Not characteristic of the app | Possible | Possible | Possible |
| **Sharing content** | Relatively easy | Not easily | Relatively easy | Relatively easy | Relatively easy |

*Source*: Re-elaboration and own translation based on Bouhnik and Deshen (2014, p. 220).

> practices with WhatsApp, but also to the forms of commitment, fidelity and knowledge that are manifested through the possibilities that are presented in this form of communication.
>
> *(O'Hara et al., 2014, p. 14)*

It is evident that from the impact of the Internet, through social networks based on network applications to the use of messaging and networks in the era of smartphones, what is found is material for social research.

In the next section, two specific examples of research carried out on and through WhatsApp and its possibilities of articulation with other options in the virtual/mobile/digital world are presented.

The examples have been selected for two different but basic reasons: the first connects teamwork, geographical relocation, and a well-known topic, while the second involves an observation experience that accompanies separation of members of the group, on a theme little known by the group, and the articulation of people located in different countries.

## 3.2 Everyday Gaze: First Experience

Everyday Gaze was an experience designed to experiment with the potential of WhatsApp as an instrument of social research. The decision to conduct the inquiry was based on at least three prior practices of our research group: a) our expertise in social conflict inquiry, b) our familiarity with participant observation and ethnography, and c) our collective experience in using WhatsApp groups.

The choice of the name reflects two assumptions of the experience: a) we wanted to explore the ways that WhatsApp offered in capturing the proximity/distance between looking/seeing/observing, and b) we wanted to carry out an experiment that would place us at the centre of the conflict in such a way that any criticism of the social phenomena could be observed.

An important component of the experiment was our belief that the phone facilitates, enhances, and amplifies the possibilities of observation. In a way that we cannot argue here, our idea of "doing an experiment" is close to the one proposed by H. Garfinkel (2006) on experiments. Creating a methodological experience is seeing an experiment as having subjects and researchers, which implies stressing the resources and skills that in one way or another are possessed or lacking.

The experience consisted of the registration/sending in and through a WhatsApp "dissemination group" in what we call a "conflict situation" from November 1 to December 1, 2016, by 13 people, all of them members of the Study Group on Sociology of Emotions and Bodies (GESEC) of the Gino Germani Research Institute of the Faculty of Social Sciences of the University of Buenos Aires.

The general idea was announced at a GESEC meeting, and once the WhatsApp group had been created, the instructions for the task were communicated through it, where text, audio, an attached document, and the sending of a message were used as information surfaces, which had the following structure:

a. WhatsApp messages
   [1/11/2016 18:15] adrianscribano: Dear friends
   [1/11/2016 18:15] adrianscribano: Today we start
   [1/11/2016 18:15] adrianscribano: Remember: observe and record
   [1/11/2016 18:15] adrianscribano: Conflictual situation
   [1/11/2016 18:16] adrianscribano: On the street, subway, bus, Facebook, Twitter, Instagram.
b. Audio 1
   Whether it's with a, well, a voice message, a video, a photo, a description, a location of the photo, at the moment it's happening on the street, on the subway, on the bus, at the moment it's going. That is important, whatever happens, in the sense of what we have been saying that this intersection between sociability, experientiality, and sensibility is an experience.
c. Document
   Scribano, Adrian. (2003). Reflections on a methodological strategy for the analysis of social protests. Sociology Magazine Federal University of Rio Grande do Sul. Institute of Philosophy and Human Sciences. Post-Graduation Program in Sociology Porto Alegre year 5 no. 9, 64–104.
d. Audio 2
   There are some things about conflict, so you can see some things that we have discussed a long time ago, but that's good… so that see this thing that I am now, we are giving it a spin under this question of a sensibility regime in the context of this normalization of enjoyment through consumption. Well, let's start working, let's see what comes out. Hugs.

The article that was sent as a theoretical reference explains in detail what conflicts, protests, and collective actions are and how to investigate them. Among many aspects of this document that are directly connected with the objectives of the inquiry that we proposed, we can highlight the following: the emergence of a "new" sociology of experience is proposed, and the notions of conflict networks are conceptualized, conflictual fields, episodes, manifestations, and conflictual expression and expressive resources.

Regarding the sociology of experience, it is stated in the document that:

> [w]ith this we are facing a particular sociology of human experience. Social action is a multipolar space; where the axes of the individual and the collective have a relationship of deep interconnection. (…) The self-recognition task produces a domain shared by the recognition mechanism of others. (…) The experience lived "with" and "of" the others in the framework of the transformations of the self generates a field of differential analysis in sociological knowledge.
>
> *(Scribano, 2003, p. 69)*

In the document, following Melucci, "'conflict is defined as that relationship between two (or more) social actors who fight for the control of resources to which both assign a value'. (Melucci 1984: 423)" (Scribano, 2003, p. 78).

In connection with the conceptualization of conflicts, conflict networks, and the conflictual field, the work used as a reference maintains that it is important to underline that what is called the conflict network here is constituted in turn by relations between actors that imply the reference to previous networks of conflict. In addition, it is proposed that a network of conflicts gives possibilities of social visibility to other networks of conflicts that, submerged or veiled, is potentially installed in daily social relations The conflict networks that manifest themselves in the protest relationally make up a multipolar space of antagonistic situations between actors in conflicts. This space, which acts as a limit and structure of the protest and as the horizon of its genesis, can be called a conflictual field. In the set of relations of attraction and rejection that the field generates, the production and reproduction of the protest are constituted.

Conflict networks, which precede and operate as a background to the protests, act over time, reconverting and redefining the positions of the agents and the meaning of the actions. Two fields are structured in permanent redefinition: the conflictual field and the negotiation field, articulated by an area of neutrality. These spaces are updated in times, in rhythms, which acquire a significant weight due to their specific value. The structuring of collective actions that have become social protests are forms of spatialization of the times in which the actors connect goals, decisions, emotional investments, and expressive resources. This spatialization can be understood if the occurrence of three moments in the protest is accepted: expression, episode, and manifestation. This is how the conceptual opportunity to capture the action in its conditions is born, that is, to be able to distinguish and interpret what happens, what is observed, and the meaning that this implies. For this, it is important to distinguish the expressions of the conflict, the manifestation of collective action, and the different episodes assumed by the aforementioned conflict networks.

In this way, Everyday Gaze is the record of *conflict situations* where the experiences of individual actors intersect with those of groups and reflect a *state of affairs* over a month.

Two hundred and thirty-two conflict situations were registered, with dissimilar problems: gender violence, distribution of social plans, cuts to education and science, lack of work, "aesthetics in the street", situations of marginality, precarious housing, pesticides, job insecurity, protests, among others.

The registration surfaces of the registry were: sending a Facebook page link, audios with descriptions of situations, photos (of graffiti, posters, mobilizations, protests, etc.), videos made with the cell phone or found in other places, messages from Twitter, links to graffiti through Google Maps, and WhatsApp texts.

Even though it is not the objective of this work, it is interesting to note that the conflict networks that emerged in and from the records do not differ much from those that we have been pointing out since the beginning of the 2000s;

they were consolidated in the last 14 years and are present today. If there is a curiosity: it is the absence of the repression of the security forces which occupied a central place in our previous records and explanations (Scribano, 2009, 2006, 2012, 2015).

WhatsApp is an instrument for developing a daily look at the social world that enables both researchers and people who perform the action to participate by expressing their emotions and sensibilities. Looking, seeing, and touching on WhatsApp connect with the impressions and perceptions of what has been received and sent, with what is photographed, recorded, and/or written, and in that line the door is opened for a recursive and permanent modality of reality.

## 3.3 Watch on WhatsApp. Methodological Strategy for a Traveling Observation

The research that feeds the content of this section has its origin in the exchanges that we are carrying out with a group of colleagues and students (Mexicans and Guatemalans), with whom we are working from the perspective of the sociology of bodies/emotions, and in our experience in the use of WhatsApp as an instrument of observation and exchange.

In what follows, we first reconstruct an approximate chronology of the march/caravan to make the journey visible, from Internet archives and the observations of the people who followed the walkers and were part of our WhatsApp group. Secondly, we reproduce two interviews with three walkers that serve as a hinge for the last part of the chapter where we will try to "open" a conclusion from this information that is a small part of what is observed and recorded.

Between October 12 and November 9, 2018, five migrant caravans were registered, while during 2019, starting in January, the departure of migrant caravans was registered again. Each caravan had the same objective of migrating in a group to support each other and avoid the difficulties of the trip. They came mainly from Honduras and El Salvador; however, along the way, they were joined by migrants from Guatemala, Mexico, and Nicaragua.

The particular group that participated in the investigation was made up of Brenda Bustos Garcia (Monterrey), Melina Amao Cenizeros (Tijuana), Eduardo Martell (Federal District, Mexico), and Jeanie Herrera (Guatemala).

The decision to use WhatsApp as an instrument of inquiry was supported by a previous experience whose "methodological" results we published under the title "Daily Views" (Scribano, 2017), where we maintained:

1. WhatsApp enables a redefinition of the connections/disconnections between observing and recording. If the agency of the researcher is taken as a permanent participant observer, the following is redefined: a) what it means to "be observing", b) "registration skills", and c) "ability to identify, select and interpret".

2. WhatsApp allows the participation of multiple observers. The existence of a permanent attitude of observation/recording on the same phenomenon by multiple observers: redefines the limits and possibilities of the relationships between different points of view; it modifies, at least partially, the relativity of those points of view by being summoned "at the same moment"; and redefines the roles and division of labour in research, horizontalizing the opportunity to "produce a look".
3. WhatsApp facilitates access to various moments of social reality, in the tension of what happens in and through the body/emotion percipient in the first person – the event narrated in a virtual way and the traces/traces of the phenomena that have already occurred in terms of a non-current flow of life.
4. Multiple edges of the social conflict are recorded when it diverges into catastrophe (*sensu* Thom). Observation via WhatsApp makes it possible to capture, at least partially, the tensions between changes and reproduction.

   Many eyes, many recording skills, many ways to access what one wants to see, and many ways of expressing the phenomenon converge in a permanent record that enhances the capture of some topologies of conflict (Scribano, 2017, p. 17).

With these people and with this methodological horizon, we set out to observe the caravan as it passed through various places, beginning in Guatemala and ending in Tijuana. The experience lasted from October 23, 2018, to November 29, 2018, and, as can be seen, involves interviews with walkers, sharing photos, videos, news, and personal feelings about what they saw or took part in.

In what follows, the exchange that gave rise to the records, their axes, and modalities is partially reproduced:

10/23/18 2:29 pm – Adrian Scribano: It seems to me that we should do something with the march of the Hondurans

10/23/ 18 2:30 pm – Adrian Scribano: Here they call it March of the Desperate
10/23/18 2:30 pm – Adrian Scribano: What do you think?

10/23/18 2:38 pm – Melina: Sounds good, here they call it Migrant Caravan. Well, I'm not an expert in the migratory issue, but I think I can make a connection between this movement (which is also handled as a diaspora) and interstitial practices, following the analytical model of research on love and collective action. But then I don't know if it's better to leave the subject I proposed and try to develop this. That the issue of trust, from the Mexican media perspective, is very peculiar because it reproduces the xenophobic speeches of the US. What do you think or suggest?

10/23/18 2:39 pm – Adrian Scribano: It seems to me that you should not leave the confidence issue aside

10/23/18 2:40 pm – Adrian Scribano: I think we can search for images, do interviews, see notes on the mass media and see social networks

10/23/18 2:41 pm – Adrian Scribano: Once we have that material we can do an analysis
10/23/18 2:44 pm – Melina: Sure, maybe everyone from their places can see how things are handled. Here in Tijuana, some shelters are already being prepared, but at the level of daily commentary, the mediated stigmas are reproduced.
10/23/18 2:45 pm – Adrian Scribano: Of course … let's each think and see
10/23/18 2:45 pm – Melina: Maybe we can make a collective email with all the addresses of who we participate with and start sharing stuff there, do like our database so to speak.
10/23/18 2:45 pm – Adrian Scribano: With Jeanie Herrera we are already doing something10/23/18 2:46 pm – Adrian Scribano: Excellent let's see what the rest think and move on later (…)
10/23/18 7:15 pm – Brenda: I also completely agree that we must do something because of the xenophobic contrast between the media, the authorities, and a good part of the population, and with another part of the population that supports and shows clear solidarity.
10/23/18 7:16 pm – Adrian Scribano: Hello people
10/23/18 7:17 pm – Adrian Scribano: My proposal is aimed at investigating and making the phenomenon critically visible, that's why it seems to me:
10/23/ 18 7:18 pm – Adrian Scribano: a) we must not look at it from "migration" because it is just the blind spot of xenophobia and miserabilism
10/23/18 7:19 pm – Adrian Scribano: b) we must give the floor to "them" trying to make us understand their silence
10/23/18 7:20 pm – Adrian Scribano: c) investigate/accompany that it may end up in a CIES Working Document with a "video"
10/23/18 7:22 pm – Adrian Scribano: I think we can "approach" them in a simple way with basic questions: a) what did they feel at home, b) what do they feel now, and c) what do they expect feel
10/23/18 7:22 pm – Brenda: It seems to me an excellent proposal not to inquire about migration
10/23/18 7:24 pm – Adrian Scribano: I think they are pilgrims, walkers, passers-by who are on journeys
10/23/18 7:25 pm – Adrian Scribano: In Africa decades ago (Rolando García wrote about this) entire villages went out in search of food, walking thousands of kilometres
10/23/18 7:26 pm – Adrian Scribano: I think we should think about how to capture these three questions in cell phone videos.

In this context, we began to accompany/record the march as it passed through the cities, using the enormous potential of the networks and the media today, always following the maxims of simplicity, listening, and openness.

As already mentioned, videos were captured, photos were taken, interviews were conducted, and information in the newspapers was followed. The following sections try to reconstruct and interpret, at least partially, what was experienced in the march/caravan.

In what follows we reproduce two interviews[1] conducted by Eduardo Martell in Mexico City that allow us to approach from the voice of the walkers a first approximation of what it felt like to walk.

The social situation that is experienced from the connection/disconnection with work is perceived as undignified and fuels the decision to walk to the United States "to have a better life".

*Interviewer:* Well, the first thing would be to ask you, what feelings did you have in your place of origin before starting the caravan?

*Interviewee 1 (E1):* No, I was already working, and the salary I earned was very little, the government did not help us, so I decided to go in the caravan to the United States to have a better life.

The journey is experienced with joy and in the story of Guatemala and Mexico take shape; they "personify" as givers, donors, and facilitators of the journey.

*Interviewer:* And, how have you felt during all this journey in the caravan, when you entered Guatemala, when you entered Mexico, afterwards? What sensations have you had throughout this journey?

*E1:* No, well, the truth, well, very well. Because in Guatemala they received us very well, they gave us food and everything, clothes and everything. The same here in Mexico. They have treated us very well, we thank Guatemala and Mexico for the good attention they have given us.

*Interviewer:* And now that you are here in Mexico City, what do you feel? How you feel?

*E1:* Well, the truth is that I feel very happy because we have already taken a very giant step, we still have to reach our own destiny. In truth, then, we thank God for being here where we are.

In this joy of advancing, God appears as a participant in how well things are going for this interviewee, and how good it has felt to be encouraged to leave. The potential arrival in the USA is experienced as a triumph and especially because it would be the same for his family, mother, and children: leave for the others, get away so that they are well.

*Interviewer:* And how do you think you will feel once you get to the place you aspire to get to? What sensations do you think you will have once you are there?

*E1:* Well, the truth would be that I would feel very good because I have succeeded for the good of my family and myself, for my mother, my children, so I think very well.

In this context, the caravan is a successful security strategy: "all united because power lies in unity".

*Interviewer:* Why travel this way in a group? That is, in this format.
*E1:* Because maybe that way together we will have a chance, the whole caravan, we will have a chance to pass. It goes, how do I say, no problem, without being attacked. Along the very dangerous road too, that's why.
*Interviewer:* I mean, is it safer to travel in a group?
*E1:* It is safer to travel in a group, yes. United all because power is in unity.

The history of sensibilities allows us to see more than interesting geopolitical twists, the path that goes from the revolutionary "the united people will never be defeated" to this union for a defensive power against coyotes, gangs, drug traffickers, and police.

The next interview, which was conducted with two people at once, reinforces what we have already been able to perceive in terms of the sensibility shared by the walkers: a) the experience of a bad life and the fantasy of a better life as triggers for the decision to leave, b) leaving is difficult and painful, c) walking is difficult, d) helping their relatives to better themselves, e) in Honduras working does not "yield" and it feels like "being in nothing", f) gratitude to the hand of God, g) in USA working can advance a person, and h) the format of the caravan is why the "union makes it stronger".

*Interviewer:* Yes, the first thing would be to know what you felt in your place of origin that made you leave? Especially that feeling.
*Interviewee 2 (E2):* The need to work, there was not much employment. We worked for three months and then they no longer gave us work. That is why it is necessary to leave our country. To improve too, to have new goals, because there in Honduras there is no work, nobody graduates. And it is very difficult for them to give you a job there in Honduras. [Interviewee 3 (E3): A decent job.] And they don't give them a decent job, there they only give a job for three months and after graduating. So no, there is not much work there.
*E3:* And also, what is it called, the payment, the minimum for the family is very little. So we decided to leave our country to overcome it, to have a new, better life.
*Interviewer:* And, what have you felt throughout this journey that you have taken during the caravan? And, what do you feel now that you are in Mexico City? What are the sensations you experience?
*E2:* When we left Honduras we felt something, leaving the family is something very difficult, very painful. Because leaving our country for another country that we do not know is very difficult. Walking, sleeping on the ground, very difficult; rain, sun, cold, hunger; hunger, well, almost not hungry, but [E3: cold] cold, tiredness, illnesses, and very difficult then.

*Interviewer:* And now that you are here in Mexico City?

*E2:* Thank God the Mexicans have helped us with food, clothing. But very, very difficult to leave our lands, but if we have an American dream, God knows what is the purpose of where we are going.

*E3:* Yes, yes, yes.

*Interviewer:* And, in that sense, what do you expect to feel at the place you want to get to? What sensations do you think you will experience once you get there?

*E2:* Well, our purpose is to see if they let us in, if Donald Trump lets us in. And, work, work, and help our family in Honduras.

*E3:* The same, work hard and help our families there, so that they can improve.

*E2:* And have a better life, well. Because in Honduras you work and you don't even have enough for your children. Only for your children. And you can't even buy a pair of shoes because there you work from seven to five in the afternoon and the most they give you is two hundred lempiras. So, it doesn't pay off, it doesn't pay off, not at all.

*Interviewer:* What sensations do you think are different between what you experienced in Honduras and what you hope to experience in the United States?

*E2:* It's different. The currency exchange is different, education, work, employment opportunity. It's something, it's different. It's one, from another, how would I say it, it's from...

*E3:* Look, the difference here in Honduras is clear, the basic food basket is through thc roof, fuel is through the roof, and a salary that doesn't pay you. So we have to nothing. And, at least, if we work there everything is more comfortable, well, so to speak. And they give him work and we can't find work there. That is why we migrated from our country.

*Interviewer:* And then, finally, why migrate in this way? Why travel this way? That is, in a group, in a caravan, with this format.

*E2:* Because there is more support, because the union makes it stronger. Because if we came alone it would be very difficult. We would not have the benefits that we have right now in the caravan that we are going in. It would be a risky thing.

*E3:* Risky, because you don't know, well, we are getting into a country that we don't know. Then anything can happen to us. We are exposed to anything.

The United States appears with the features of a social fantasy where it is a place that sutures the breaks and failures of another place, a space where "there is" what is not in Honduras. A place where problems are "magically" solved after making the sacrifice of walking.

## 3.4 Consequences and Learning

When a mobile device is used every day at all hours as an instrument to identify, record, and report, a series of "effects" are produced, in the face of which we must always have a reflective attitude as central parts of the findings themselves and our ways of interpreting the world. Among the different consequences of our experience, we have chosen to emphasize that WhatsApp enables a redefinition of the connections/disconnections between observing and recording, allows the participation of multiple observers, and facilitates access to various moments of social reality in terms of the tensions of "lived worlds" and the registration of multiple edges of the social conflict.

### 3.4.1 WhatsApp Enables a Redefinition of the Connections/ Disconnections between Observing and Recording

If the researcher's agency is taken as a *permanent participant observer*, the following is redefined: a) what it means to "be observing", b) "registration skills", and c) "ability to identify, select, and interpret".

a) In this way, the notion of immanent criticism and location of the researcher in a position of double hermeneutics is modified; researchers live during conflicts but academia persists in denying the radical intersubjectivity of the objectivity of looking critically, b) the skills of the subject are redirected in terms of scientific systematicity. Learning to use the cell phone is its "smart" trait implies improving the capacity for inquiry (photo, video, voice, and writing) in a simultaneous act of daily life that becomes life-in-research, and c) the simultaneous seeing/ registering improves the possibilities of "finding" what is sought in what exists in said act of theoretical/epistemic/methodological articulation, the imputation of meaning is facilitated and expanded.

### 3.4.2 WhatsApp Allows the Participation of Multiple Observers

The existence of a permanent state of observation/recording of the same phenomenon by multiple observers redefines the limits and possibilities of the relationships between different points of view, and modifies, at least partially, the relativity of those points of view when they are summoned "at the same moment" and redefines the roles and division of labour in research, horizontalizing the opportunity to "produce a look".

### 3.4.3 Facilitates Access to Various Moments of Social Reality

This occur in the tension of what happens in and through the body and perceiving emotion; the event is narrated in a virtual way, and the traces of the phenomena have already occurred in terms of a non-current life flow. At least since the beginning of the 2000s, for people who are not condemned to existence in expulsion, the spread of the virtual has allowed them to take part in a different kind of reality. Life in the virtual world was added to face-to-face life and temporal-spatial disembedding: a finger-to-finger life due to the important role of the fingertips and hands in this new audio-visual world. It is precisely in this multilevel occurrence of a plurality of integrated spheres of the same experience that sensibilities and sociability are modified.

### *3.4.4 Multiple Edges of the Social Conflict Are Registered*

This occurs in its divergence into catastrophe (*sensu* René Thom). Observation via WhatsApp makes it possible to capture, at least partially, the tensions between changes and reproductions. It also allows us to understand how the use of applications such as these disproves that the real perceived here and now is one of the possibilities of multiple divergences that, in the heat of a sensation of infinity, "creates" the conviction of the impossibility of recording. The radical material construction of reality is stripped bare in terms of the possibilities of capturing flow/reproduction/change at the same time.

Many eyes, many recording abilities, many accesses to what one wants to see, and many ways of expressing the phenomenon converge in a permanent record that enhances the capture of some topologies of conflict.

Like any experience, like anything done to start a new path, the use of WhatsApp is a reminder of and renews old-new problems in the social sciences as sciences. A voice of many voices, various narrations of various silences, the use of WhatsApp is a possibility to reopen a space of old listening with new vehicles.

## Note

1 We thank Paula Zanini for the transcription of the interviews.

## References


Ahad, A. D., & Lim, S. M. A. (2014). Convenience or nuisance?: The 'WhatsApp' dilemma. *Procedia-Social and Behavioral Sciences, 155*, 189–196.

Bouhnik, D., & Deshen, M. (2014). WhatsApp goes to school: Mobile instant messaging between teachers and students. *Journal of Information Technology Education: Research, 13*, 217–231. http://www.jite.org/documents/Vol13/JITEv13ResearchP217-231Bouhnik0601.pdf

Bryson, A., Gomez, R., & Willman, P. (2010). Online social networking and trade union membership: what the Facebook phenomenon truly means for labor organizers. *Labor history, 51*(1), 41–53.

Cingolani, P. (2016). Capitalismo de plataforma: nuevas tecnologías de la comunicación e internacionalización del trabajo. *Boletín Onteaiken, 22*, 42–47.

De Sena, A., & Lisdero, P. (2015). Etnografía Virtual: aportes para su discusión y diseño. In De Sena, A., (Comp.), *Caminos cualitativos: aportes para la investigación en Ciencias Sociales*, (pp. 71–100). CICCUS- Imago Mundi.

Fernández, I., & Del Barrio Fernández, A. (2017). Hábitos de uso del Whatsapp por parte de los adolescentes. *International Journal of Developmental and Educational Psychology, 2*(1), 23–30.

Fuchs, Ch. (2016). Trabajo Digital e Imperialismo. *Boletín Onteaiken, 22*, 32–41.

Garfinkel, H. (2006). *Estudios en Etnometodología*. Anthropos Editorial.

Guiñez-Cabrera, N. A., & Mansilla-Obando, K. (2021). WhatsApp Web con fines académicos en tiempos de la covid-19. *Apertura, 13*(2), 54–69.

Lansen, A., & Garcia, A. (2015). '. . . but I haven't got a body to show': Self-pornification and male mixed feelings in digitally mediated seduction practices. *Sexualities, 18*(5/6), 714–730.

Lisdero, P. (2010). Call centers: Comunicación, Tecnología y Trabajo. Hacia una propuesta interpretativa de las expropiaciones de las energías corporales en contextos de Neo-Colonialidad. In *La llamada... El Trabajo y los trabajadores de Call Centers en Córdoba* (pp. 67–95). Universitas – Editorial Científica Univesitaria.

Losada Díaz, J. C., & Zamora Medina, R. (2021). Nuevos escenarios para la conversación política: el uso de WhatsApp por parte de los partidos durante la campaña electoral de abril de 2019 en España. *Palabra Clave, 24*(1), 1–28.

Martínez Rolán, X., & Piñeiro Otero, T. (2017). El uso de los memes en la conversación política 2.0 una aproximación a una movilización efímera. *Prisma Social, 18*, 55–84.

O'Hara, K., Massimi, M., Harper, R., Rubens, S., & Morris, J. (2014). Everyday dwelling with WhatsApp. In Conference: Proceedings of the 17th ACM conference on Computer Supported Cooperative Work & Social Computing. https://doi.org/10.1145/2531602.2531679.

Piaia, V., & Alves, M. (2020). Abrindo a caixa preta: análise exploratória da rede bolsonarista no WhatsApp. *Intercom: Revista Brasileira de Ciências da Comunicação, 43*(3), 135–154.

Romero Oliva, C., Montilla Coronado, M. del V. C., Pazos Gómez, M., & Martín Montilla, A. (2016). Una modalidad actual de violencia de género en parejas de jóvenes: las redes sociales. *Educación XX1, 19*(2), 405–429.

Rubio-Romero, J., & Perlado Lamo de Espinosa, M. (2015). El fenómeno *WhatsApp* en el contexto de la comunicación personal: una aproximación a través de los jóvenes universitarios. *Icono, 14*(13), 73–94. https://doi.org/10.7195/ri14.v13i2.818

Scribano, A. (2003). Reflexiones sobre una estrategia metodológica para el análisis de las protestas sociales. *Sociologías. Universidade Federal do Rio Grande do Sul, 5*(9), 64–104.

Scribano, A. (2006). Cuando las Aguas Bajan: La Mirada de los pobres sobre las consecuencias de la crisis argentina del 2001 en la Ciudad de Córdoba. In C. Masse Narváez, (Coord.), *Poderes Locales y Desarrollo Municipal. Actores Sociales e Institucionales* (pp. 139–160). IEEM UAEM.

Scribano, A. (2009). "Más acá" de las demandas: Un mapeo preliminar de las acciones colectivas en Argentina 2003–2007. *Controversias y Concurrencias Latinoamericanas, 1*(1), 179–199.

Scribano, A. (2012). Interdicciones colectivas, violencia y movimientos sociales, hoy. *Revista Actuel Marx/Intervenciones, 13*, 19–39.

Scribano, A. (2015). Notas sobre conflictos, acciones colectivas, protestas y movimientos sociales a principios de un siglo. *Boletín Onteaiken, 20*, 1–7.

Scribano, A. (2017). Miradas cotidianas. El uso de Whatsapp como experiencia de investigación social. *Revista Latinoamericana de Metodología de la Investigación Social, 13*(7), 8–22.

Simply Measuerd. (2016). *The State of Social Marketing*. 2016 Report. Retrieved from https://irishtechnews.ie/the-state-of-social-marketing-in-2016-from-simply-measured-reviewed-by-gus-ryan/

Tresáncoras, A. G., Piqueras, J. A. & García-Oliva, C. (2017). Relación del uso problemático de WhatsApp con la personalidad y la ansiedad en adolescentes. *Salud y drogas, 17*(1), 27–36.

Williams, J. P. (2009). Community, frame of reference and boundary: Three sociological concepts and their relevance for virtual worlds research. *Qualitative Sociology Review, V*(2), 3–16.

Zumárraga-Espinosa, M. (2021). WhatsApp, comunicación móvil y participación política: un estudio cuantitativo en Ecuador. *Contratexto, 35*, 17–42.

# 4

# POLITICS AND LOVE

## Two Digital Ethnographies

## Introduction

Society 4.0 implies an increase in the life lived by subjects in mobile/digital/virtual settings and with this, the challenge for the social sciences is to systematize observation processes of that daily life. Traditional ethnography, observation, and various forms of participatory research allowed the social sciences to have the necessary resources to consider new observation devices. Digital ethnography (DE) is particularly presented as an inquiry device through which sensibilities and emotions are captured.

This chapter outlines the central features of digital ethnographies: a) facilitating a conceptual approach that allows understanding the basic concepts of the device, b) synthesizing two examples of research carried out, and finally, c) presenting some theoretical and epistemological features of DE in conclusion.

This chapter seeks to discuss the belief that researching on the Internet is a mere *looking at web pages* and that immersion in the virtual/mobile/digital world cannot be considered ethnography. From an emphatically sociological point of view, the chapter was designed to share with readers the conviction that traveling *to the digital* implies a profound form of ethnography where sensibilities are observed, emotions are spread, and where the researcher's emotional ecologies are brought into play.

## 4.1 Digital Ethnography: Some Theoretical Considerations

One of this book's central purposes, especially this chapter, is to emphasize how virtual/mobile/digital inquiry devices capture sensibilities. In this context, it is important to point out how DE is frequently used today, and on many occasions, the reports of these practices include experiences, sensations, emotions, affections, and sensibilities.

DOI: 10.4324/9781003319771-5

Castillo-Torres et al. (2019) propose that an ethnography of the virtual world within *game studies* forms a specific part of cultural studies where, among other aspects, experiences and emotions are mapped.

On the other hand, Laura Leon (2018) concludes her work on child YouTubers and the video creation process – evidence of transmedia skills in action – affirming that "the evidence speaks to us of a different experience and sensibility, lived within the contemporary collaborative culture" (p. 118).

De Sena (2011) in her work "Colours and forms: towards a methodology for the investigation of the Internet. Sociology and advertising on the Web" explores the interaction between sensations, media, and virtuality.

Fifteen years ago, Beer and Burrows (2007) pointed out how the digital world was becoming increasingly important for the mundane routines of daily life, and in that context they discussed some of the ways to interact with what at that time were new web applications and called for the development of a sociological understanding of the new digital cultures.

For social research from different perspectives (both theoretical and disciplinary), the Internet is today a widely used source (Williams, 2009; Sloan & Quan-Haase, 2017; Botin & Børsen, 2021). Many processes, strategies, and tools are implemented currently through the Internet: an investigation through blogs (LaBanca, 2011; Chenail, 2011a), virtual ethnography (Domínguez et al., 2007), semi-structured interviews (Al-Saagaf & Williamson, 2004), and the use of YouTube (Chenail, 2011b), to mention just some.

There are a serics of studies that reflect on the meaning and use of YouTube and video clip channels in everyday life in general, and in social investigation in particular: Díaz Arias (2009), Artero (2010), Pérez Rufí and Gómez Pérez (2010), and Mera and Therón (2009). In the same vein, we can observe a set of studies on Facebook (Berlanga & Martínez, 2010); on cyber language and rhetoric, (Piscitelli, 2009); about promises of virtual worlds, referred to their impact on labour organizations (Bryson, Gomez, & Willman, 2010); or in their relation to the capacity for identity and community formation (Papacharissi, 2009). Regarding Twitter, there are already manuals for its application in social investigation, such as that of Bernal (2013) and Reilly (2011); articles in specialized magazines on specific topics such as that of Fenge, Hodges, and Cutts (2011) about a participative methodology using Twitter as a tool; or the work of Huberman et al. (2008) on its potentialities as a social network. This chapter has as a basis the methodological strategy that Daniel Domínguez Figaredo (2007) has criticized regarding DE and what Christine Hine (2004) has systematized in her book on ethnography in digital contexts.

Digital and/or virtual ethnography can be defined in various ways, among others as shown by Mosquera:

> Cyberspace and cyberculture make adoption necessary of Cyber-anthropology and with it the birth of Ethnography of the cyberculture in new ethnographies called Cyberethnography… Ethnography of Cyberspace… Virtual Ethnography… Anthropology of Media… Mediated

> Ethnography… Ethnography from/in/through the Internet… all of them as a diversity of names for what in this work is called digital ethnography, but that in Internet studios is better known as 'virtual ethnography'.
>
> *(Mosquera, 2008, p. 541)*

In another vein, Jörgen Skågeby, trying to give a first approximation of the basic components of online ethnography, has written that:

> The online ethnographical procedure consists of a number of different steps, namely cultural entrance (or entrée), collection and analysis of data while also making sure that trustworthy interpretations are made, conducting ethically sound research and making sure that members of the studied milieu can provide feedback to the research(er). This chapter will describe these steps, but use a slightly different, and elaborated taxonomy, i.e. defining setting and research perspective; making an entrance; qualitative online data collection; analysis; and presentation of results. Additionally, the author will also consider the omnipresent ethical dilemmas that colour online ethnographical research.
>
> *(Skågeby, 2010, p. 411)*

From yet another perspective, Sarah Pink and her colleagues in the introduction to her book *Digital Ethnography: Principles and Practice* argue:

> Digital Ethnography outlines an approach to doing ethnography in a contemporary world. It invites researchers to consider how we live and research in a digital, material and sensory environment. This is not a static world or environment. Rather, it is one in which we need to know how to research in it as it develops and changes. Digital Ethnography also explores the consequences of the presence of digital media in shaping the techniques and processes through which we practice ethnography, and accounts for how the digital, methodological, practical and theoretical dimensions of ethnographic research are increasingly intertwined.
>
> *(Pink et al., 2016, p. 19)*

In her influential work, Christine Hine (2015) makes an approach to DE based on understanding the Internet as an embedded, embodied, and everyday phenomenon/space.

> First, I outline the grounds for thinking of the Internet as an embedded phenomenon. The Internet is often not experienced as a transcendent "cyberspace" in contemporary society, but has become something which is embedded into people's lives in ways which are meaningful within specific contexts (Bakardjieva, 2005). This embedded Internet poses a methodological challenge in that the frames of meaning-making which

> the ethnographer is required to pursue are initially unpredictable, often diverse, and can require considerable agility of method and mobility of focus. Second, I turn to the embodied Internet. Again, rather than being a transcendent cyberspatial site of experience, the Internet has increasingly become a part of us. Often we do not think of "going online" as a discrete form of experience, but we find ourselves being online in an extension of other embodied ways of being and acting in the world. This section will explore the extent to which experience of the online environment has become seamlessly integrated with other embodied experiences. I also reflect on the tensions between the public portrayal of a universal "Internet" and the very personalized experiences we may have, using Tsing's work on the friction between the universal and the specific (Tsing, 2005). The methodological challenge is to recognize the consequent diversity and highly personal nature of the online experience, suggesting a shift towards recognition of the ontological diversity of the Internet and an embrace of reflexive and autoethnographic methods as a valuable component of a virtual ethnography.
>
> *(Hine, 2015, p. 14)*

This view of Hine is very relevant to the objectives of this book for its consideration of the embodiment of the virtual/mobile/digital world.

In her study on digital sociology, Deborah Lupton already points out that DE and the set of associated digital practices complicate the structure of observation within the framework of the modifications of traditional strategies of inquiry.

> Ethnographic research, particularly as undertaken by anthropologists, has contributed major insights into how people in various cultural and geographical locations use digital technologies. However, the very ubiquity and dispersal of new digital devices have challenged traditional notions of ethnographic research. Given the dispersal of the internet across many different types of device, platforms and tool, and the complex relationship between "the online" and "the offline" worlds, the notion of undertaking fieldwork as a participant-observer in a specific and well-defined "field site" has become problematised.
>
> *(Lupton, 2015, p. 50)*

This constitutes a horizon of understanding how multiple bands of the same Mobius strip are configured, where devices, technologies, and applications mutually influence each other, configuring fields of inquiry.

Inscribed in this horizon of multiplicity and complexity, the description of Domínguez and his colleagues is better understood:

> Current approaches in the ethnographic study of the Internet are diverse; the proliferation of proposals has been numerous in recent years. The

> methodological approach of virtual ethnography has been broadened and reformulated through new proposals such as digital ethnography, ethnography on/of/through the Internet, connective ethnography, networked ethnography, cyberethnography, etc. Each of these maintains its own dialogue with the established tradition of ethnography and formulates its relation to this tradition in different ways.
>
> *(Domínguez et al., 2007, p. 1)*

As recently synthesized by Sandberg and Rossi (2021), in this century, social research has increased its practices in virtual environments in such a way that new forms of collection, storage, and analysis have appeared that have transformed and expanded the paths of inquiry.

> The computational turn within social science and digital humanities has proliferated new data formats and not least new questions for research (Boellstorff and Maurer, 2015; Blok and Pedersen, 2014). Whereas the so-called "big data" refer to data accessed on the basis of computational social science methods through API or data scrapings from social media platforms such as Facebook and Twitter, ethnographic materials are generated on the basis of qualitative research methods and ethnographic fieldwork, including in-situ engagements like participating observations, face-to-face conversations, in-depth semi-structured interviews, and online "netnography" (Kozinets, 2019).
>
> *(Sandberg & Rossi, 2021, p. 3)*

It is precisely Kozinets who emphasized the qualities of netnography in one of the aspects that this book wants to highlight: digital strategies are committed to "participatory-observational humanistic research" and therefore are as ethnographic, participatory, and humanistic as the modalities of "face to face".

> The nature of contemporary netnography is that of "a specific set of related data collection, analysis, ethical and representational research practices", where a significant amount of the data is collected through a very humanist participant-observational research stance (Kozinets, 2015, p. 79). This is ethnographic research conducted within and upon the new time-spatial cultural coordinates mediated by contemporary networked communications, such as the Internet and the variety of devices and forms that humans use to access it. Many research methods focus on the Internet, the devices, and the technologies with which it is associated. Not netnography. Humanism, attention to the details and contexts of human stories and human understandings, of people using technologies, is the hallmark of genuine netnography, just as attention to human detail distinguished all ethnographies from all non-ethnographies.
>
> *(Kozinets, 2021, p. 3)*

Recently, Lodi and Scanio (2021), in their work on digital anthropology in Argentina, have synthesized in the following way the netnography features:

> Netnography is presented as a new qualitative research methodology that adapts classical ethnographic techniques to the study of cultures and communities emerging from computer-mediated communications (CMO). In both cases, the ethnographic procedures that help shape researchers' participant observation are equivalent and include: (1) entering the field, (2) collecting and analyzing data, (3) ensuring reliable interpretation, (4) conduct ethical research, and (5) provide opportunities for feedback from community members. Within its instruments we can include both participant observation and web crawling, tag clouds, sentiment analysis, PageRank and other algorithms, semantic analysis, social network analysis, etc.
>
> *(Lodi & Scanio, 2021, p. 133)*

In this context, it is possible to observe the appearance of mobile ethnography with the proposal of a specific application to carry out the work of immersion, participation, and monitoring.

> With the convergence of smartphones, video, 4G networks and social networking/messaging, mobile ethnography (sometimes referred to as "Digital Ethnography") has emerged as an increasingly popular autoethnographic research methodology. (…) Mobile ethnography utilizes an App installed on the respondent's smartphone that enables respondents to record their everyday lives in relation to the topic of research being undertaken.
>
> *(Murphy, 2022, p. 8)*

As we will see in the next chapter on the use of drones, DE also has the characteristic feature of enabling the participation of all those who share the digital neighbourhood that is being shared, one of those ways of inhabiting a digital time/space is that of citizen participation as investigated by Birkbak et al., and in their work "Digital methods contributions to citizen hearings: A techno-anthropological approach to Twitter and Technology Assessment" maintain:

> In short, digital methods come with specific sensitivities (e.g. to media specificity) and a specific conceptualisation of publics (as not falling clearly on any one side of a lay vs. expert divide). This also means that a particular take on participation has been cultivated in relation to digital methods (Marres, 2017). These developments owe not least to how the wider relevance of controversy mappings has been shown to depend on participatory processes involving those engaged in the controversies being mapped.
>
> *(Birkbak et al., 2021, p. 112)*

Banhishikha Ghosh in her article "Digital Ethnography during the Covid-19 pandemic", following Cocq argues that doing DE involves addressing three basic questions:

1. Where: the first step is to identify the location from where the researcher wants to collect data.
2. How: the second step is to decide the selection of interlocutors. Such choices and the patterns of selection should be linked to research objectives.
3. Who: finally, the researcher should locate the interlocutor and make him/her aware of the objectives of research and thereby addresses issues of ethics and ownership.

*(Gosh, 2020)*

In the same vein, Gosh maintains "that identifying the routes and places (the *where*), the value of documentation (the *how*) and the key role of research subjects (the *who*) are therefore primary to do digital ethnographic research" (Gosh, 2020).

Following Markham (2020), it is possible to recognize the following "history" of social science online research thought as waves of "cyber-events" that, from our perspective, arm the mode of digital knowledge production and that this book reflects in various ways:

**Wave 1, early–mid 1990s: Cyberspace** – in the early and mid-1990s, when the internet was new for most people, researchers were focused on (dis)embodiment, identity, geographically dispersed community, and matters of virtuality. No wonder: all these ways of being in the world and with others were accomplished through the exchange of texts in various shared spaces online.

**Wave 2, early 2000s: Web 2.0 and the age of sharing** – the early 2000s were characterized by the return of the social web but in markedly different ways than the sociality of the early 1990s. Here, rapid growth of software for interaction via the web created greater possibilities for commenting, writing back, and otherwise giving feedback to information that was being posted.

**Wave 3, Mid-late 2000s: Platformization of social networking** – Myspace, Facebook, Sina Weibo, YouTube, Twitter, Instagram. While not the first, these platforms represent how expression, interaction, networking, and sharing could be combined in a single online service.

**Wave 4, early 2010s: The rise of big data** – in 2011, several events are remarkable because their impact was felt globally through social media: the floods in Queensland, Australia; earthquakes in Christchurch, New Zealand; the Japanese earthquake, tsunami, and nuclear disaster; and the Arab Spring, which was most widely represented on social media by journalists on the ground during the Tunisian and Egyptian uprisings.

**Wave 5, mid-late 2010s: Algorithms, predictive analytics, and more than human relations** – following the surge of interest in big data analytics, the use of automated data collection and analysis tools, social research of the digital has turned again, to consider what it means to live in a world that is data-driven and where machine learning creates automated analysis of who we are and what we (will) do.

*(Markham, 2020, p. 8)*

On the horizon of what I have proposed so far, it is understandable how this chapter within the framework of the book may propose that DE is a device to capture sensibilities for reasons of the historical development of the virtual/mobile/digital world and for the guidelines that have been established in recent years about DE.

## 4.2 Digital Ethnographies, Two Experiences

As in the entire book, two examples of DE directed by the writer are presented below as a synthetic presentation of two concrete experiences so that the reader perceives some of its general features of it. The ethnography on love as collective action was carried out in six Latin American countries in 2016 and 2017 and the one referring to politics in Argentina in 2015 and 2016.

### *4.2.1 Digital Ethnography of Love*

Our research on love aims to occupy a different place from the spacing elaborated by the visions of romantic love (Giddens), from the view of love as a trap of patriarchalism (Ahmed), and the very roots of power and domination (Foucault). Love between men and women has indeed been used, at different times in history, as a tool of invisibility, exploitation, and dogmatism (Federici, Lugones), but in this work, you will find an oblique perspective that denies those expropriatory and discriminatory practices.

Our focus here is intersectional, where gender, age, ethnicity, and plural subjective dispositions are configured in their hermeneutical starting point.

It is obvious that throughout the book we use the name of the country as a collective and universal denomination to represent a heterogeneous, plural, and changing reality. The use of this name does not forget the inequalities, differences, and colonialities that they imply but that for the sake of convenience we chose to use.

In the recent literature on love, it is possible to find a diversity of empirical research, theoretical reflections, and epistemic and methodological approaches. Love in its pluri-semantic character, in the multiple practices to which it alludes, and its geo-cultural dependence is approached in many different ways. It is investigated in association with the "family" and every form of daily coexistence, from sexualities and genders, to affective bonds, just to mention some. Each of these modalities alludes to one of the multiple sides of social practice with a contingent and variable geometry.

Among the many that can be mentioned: the online love of university students (Steers et al., 2016), a critical look at love as a "meeting" (Lamy, 2016), a psychoanalytic exploration of the objects of love (Pellegrini, 2016), a neurocognitive approach to the place of tears (crying) of children and adults about maternal love (Riem et al., 2017), the place of love in moral judgments (Magid & Schulz, 2017), love as a motor of care (Pulcini, 2017), and research on the influence of the perceived risk of ending a romantic relationship in the intensity of romantic affect (Sciara & Pantaleo, 2018).

There is also an important group of works oriented to discussing some aspects of the relationship between emotions and love specifically. Malinowska and Gratzke (2018) analyze, among other topics, the relationship between love, objects, and forms of materializing affection, wondering how affections are "embodied" in objects and social relationships. Halwani (2010) is oriented to the discussion of connections between love and sexuality from a perspective of moralities and their implications for society.

Inglis (2013) offers a portrait of how love is inscribed in capitalism from an intimate perspective that asks about the bridges between love, care, and individualistic society. Seebach (2017) aims to explore how love and society connect, based on the fact that desire and the search for love is something that we share with almost all members of society from the perspective of the sociology of emotions and the sociology of morality (Pratesi, 2017). Although it is concerned about the care and solidarity among human beings, this book takes the energies of families as a starting point to show this "other" face of care.

One point in common beyond the obvious differences between these inquiries is the abandonment of an "abstract" and/or romantic view of love to take it up again as a practice that crosses the complex web of interactions between human beings. Love implies action and demands answers, not substantial or dogmatic, but it opens the field of the possibility of reciprocity, or its absence, in the connections between people.

This research on filial love as collective action has been undertaken across six countries thanks to the collaboration of young colleagues who have given us their selfless support: Melina Amao Ceniceros (Mexico), Jeanie Herrera (Guatemala), Joziene Ferraz de Assis (Brazil), Sharon Díaz (Uruguay), and Rafael Arriaza Peña (Chile).

The methodological strategy consisted of developing a DE based on: a) the development of three types of records: virtual field notes, selection and analysis of relevant moments in the life of the groups, and description of content and analysis of documents available on the Internet. These were useful to reconstruct the particularities and differences in each one of the components of the web pages and the news of the social networks on the groups investigated, and b) DE, carried out in six countries of Latin America: Mexico, Guatemala, Brazil, Uruguay, Chile, and Argentina. The research covers a large group of collective practices (more than 100) that have or have had a presence on the Internet and whose social experience has been installed since the 1970s to the present. The records were rendered into two types of tables. They were systematized by decade/year of collective creation, description of the practice, logo/image/drawing used as social identity, members, and years.

The process of DE can be understood as consisting of four consecutive but (and fundamentally) dialectical activities: 1. progressive approach, 2. systematic recording, 3. systematization, and 4. analysis/interpretation.

1. The progressive approach can be understood if it is thought of as a process for which, in the first instance, it is necessary to visualize/navigate the possibilities of the space/field of observation; then the network or immersion surface is selected according to the problem studied, and finally the actors and agents involved with the research problem are identified.
2. On the other hand, systematic registration implies: the use of record resources (tables, digital instruments), the elaboration of records according to the dimensions/variables of the research, and the design and execution of different record surfaces.
3. The systematization involves a tensional game between classification, organization, and articulation/connection between the observations and experiences of the subjects involved. From here they visualize, and connect the objects, narrations, and interactions that make up the world of digital life.
4. The analysis/interpretation game should be approached from the dialectic between recursion, continuous immersion, and native-hermeneutic.

It is in this theoretical-methodological framework that the ethnography carried out was framed, keeping always in mind the differences in academic formation, theoretical perspectives, and the geopolitical situation of the ethnographers in each country.

It is in this way that we seek to make a small contribution to the efforts to link values, virtues, and scientific knowledge of society, emphasizing the possibilities that digital offers for this. We seek to contribute a grain of sand so that it is understood that, as opposed to the immediate enjoyment of consumption and the distrust in societies of the 21st century, are realized social practices based on love and the pursuit of happiness.

### *4.2.2 Digital Politics*

All of this book is founded, in a global sense, on the convergence of critical theory, critical hermeneutics, and critical-dialectic realism on one hand, and the encounter between the sociology of body/emotions, ideology criticism, and studies of collective action and social conflict, on the other. But more specifically it is based on the discussions and studies referring to the connections between spectacle/emotions/politics and the market. It is a particular proposal to understand the politics of emotions from a methodological perspective that recovers and elaborates what we know so far about research on and through the Internet.

"Classical" literature about spectacle and social structuration has given a special place to the relations between technologies, politics, and emotions. Debord, Bataille, and Baudrillard are the most recognized authors in this field and in one way or another operate as a horizon of comprehension of what is written in this chapter. Furthermore, it is inevitable that the multiple and diverse contributions of the critical theory of the Frankfurt School are mentioned – from the connections between enlightenment and mass society (Horkheimer and Adorno) – through the thoughts on sensibilities and technique (Benjamin, Bloch) up to the studies on authoritarianism, personality structure, and industrial society (Adorno, Marcuse, Fromm) that set the basis for a critical look at the "production of sensibilities". In the same direction, we must mention the investigations of media, politics, and spectacle by Kellner (2002) and Langman (2002) on spectacularization and carnivalization of politics. Also significant are the works of Moshe and Amir (2003) on "pseudo-events" and media, Roberts (2003) on "typologies of spectacle", Bañuelos (2009) in his article "YouTube as a platform of spectacle society", Briceño Alcaraz (2001) on body and society in spectacle, and Gau and James (2013) about spectacle in sports, among many others. In this line, social studies of emotions have also been the object of diverse treatments from Darwin, through Sartre, and arriving at the proposals of Collins, Hochschild, Kemper, Illouz, and Scheff, just to mention some of the most recognized reference points. There are also disciplinary and thematic approximations (for studies on both bodies and emotions), such as, for example, Csordas (1994) (embodiment) and Ingold (2000) (materiality and skill) in anthropology, and those of James Jasper (2011) and Helena Flam (2004) related to the connections between emotions and collective action.

A central aspect of what is presented here is the methodological strategy used: virtual ethnography.

The methodological strategy consisted of developing a virtual ethnography based on the following postulations: a) the approach to what I have called the "Spectacle for Everyone" has been partial, progressive, and contingent, and b) I have elaborated four types of records: virtual field notes, selection and analysis of relevant moments, description of the content, and analysis of documents available on the Internet. Virtual field notes were useful to reconstruct the particularities and differences in each of the components of the government's social networks (GSN); the selection and analysis of moments (objects/processes) allowed us to identify the central elements of the staging that took place in the GSN; the description of contents was oriented to highlight the features of the GSN as constructors of a "spectacle for everyone"; and the analysis of documents allowed the incorporation of key information to understand the components of action that the GSN takes for granted.

Given the complexity, density, and volume of the networks that form the GSN, this chapter discusses only some of our findings to offer a better justification and evidence for our interpretation. The order of the analytical expositions is through a sequence, even though the notes and analytical process have been complex and interconnected.

In this manner, the official YouTube channel, the Football for Everyone (FFE) web page, Twitter, and the official presidential Facebook page were used as key pieces of a puzzle that could offer an idea, approximate at least, of how the relations between politics, social networks, market, and spectacle were built.

As in all ethnography, the prevailing attitude has been that of an outsider/stranger who intends to discover and comprehend the world in and through what is expressed, told, and dramatized by the inhabitants of that world. But the visitor also includes his emotions, his theories, and the images of the world that lie in them. It is important to remark that given the goal of the present chapter, the perceptions surrounding the GSN and their relation with the elaboration of the sensibilities that I have underlined here are the most relevant for such purposes.

## 4.3 By Way of Conclusion

DE is a more than an adequate strategy to capture sensibilities for various reasons, among which it is important to emphasize: its quality of cognitive/affective experience, the multidimensionality of what is perceived/recorded/interpreted, and its "natural" moment/surface of expressiveness.

DE is an investigative experience that resembles the process of getting to know a neighbourhood that we have never seen before: you have to enter alert and attentive, you have to talk to the people you sense to be "representative", you have to find out where they buy the food, you have to learn the vernacular institutions, know what to do in crisis contexts, etc. When one "arrives" at an Instagram identity and begins to follow it, we do (almost unthinkingly) this, we recognize the landscape, the people, and the narratives. Following this same line, we must decide if we take notes, record audios, prepare to write "later", ask the other objects to "support" observations (newspapers, booklets, albums), or "recover" the narratives of the comments we are witnessing, to see how it is done in that particular world –virtual/mobile/digital.

Following an influencer, subscribing to a page or newsletter, and commenting on the Facebook wall involves a triple activity of seeing, analyzing, and expressing, which as a practice have the same "structure" online and offline.

Daily life based on thoughtlessness, iteration, and the balance between reliability and risk (*sensu* Giddens) in the conditions of a normalized society in immediate enjoyment through consumption enthrones and consecrates the imperative of having experiences as one of the outstanding features of the social structure. No one "really" lives if they don't have novel, particular, personalized, and intense experiences. The virtual/mobile/digital world is a vehicle, factory, and place to store and sell experiences.

In the above context, DE as an observation practice also becomes a cognitive/affective experience that is structured based on the capture of expressed sensibilities.

To better understand DE as an experience, it is possible to approach it from a perspective focused on the process and secondly from the position of the person who performs the ethnography.

DE as a process is a systematic, designed, open, and complex experience where the observer "goes testing a state of affairs". It is *systematic* because the researcher captures the multiplicity, reordering according to theoretical criteria, native sensibility, and empirical recurrences according to the research problem/objective connection. The tension between these ways of ordering what is experienced produces the sensations of capturing virtual/mobile/digital reality. It is *designed* because when immersing in the "day to day" that is necessary to understand the very virtual/mobile/digital structure of the phenomenon, it is necessary to elaborate cartographies with flexible but essential designs where the expressive dimensions of the experienced world are included, logs are put together. From a journey with an uncertain end, compasses are built to guide the walk. It is *open* because it never dogmatizes, moralizes, or enshrines goals, processes, or assumptions, producing a set of folds and unfolds. It is in this sense that the digital ethnographic practice is being carried out, observing is observed, the conditions of observation have the logic of a continuous flow, and they are lands that are always under exploration. And it is *complex* because it includes the visual, the auditory, the tactile, and the various inscription surfaces narrated in the virtual/mobile/digital world, observing where relationality and reciprocity characterize its structure and incidentally.

DE from the position of the observer is an experience of inclusion, commitment, listening, and response. Access to a virtual/mobile/digital world puts and predisposes the observer to a position and disposition to request *inclusion*, be included according to rules, and/or perform the actions with the people who share that world with us.

From (already prehistoric) web pages, through blogs, to messaging applications, there are formal (or informal) mechanisms for subscription, membership, and/or monitoring of the group, institution, movement, and/or related company with the problem addressed. As in all ethnography, managing inclusion in the stories of a particular community is one of the most difficult positions for those who observe that "being there" is a way of "being there" and for this, we need to include ourselves (even in rejection). The other characteristic of the disposition of the person who carries out the ethnography is the *commitment* to the objectives of the collective that the virtual/mobile/digital world being observed supposes.

Commitment implies remaining willing to be in that world, giving guarantees of the will to cooperate, manifesting the ability to keep the word/action, and building mutual trust. The commitment is the strength of the continuity of the action to get to know more about the problem and the community. On the other hand, ethnography is attentive, prolonged, and unstructured listening. The sociology of attention and listening go hand in hand, and DE is a great act of listening that aims to identify, manage, and interact with the moments and spaces that a virtual/mobile/digital world opens, demanding attention. Listening as attention is an act of intentionality open to the claims of sensibility established by others. Finally, DE is also *a response* sought and offered in the virtual/mobile/digital world, responding is the result of attention-listening, responding is committing to an act according to what is heard, and it is to commit again.

In DE, whoever observes responds to the motivations, intentions, and objectives of those who create the virtual/mobile/digital world that they are sharing.

In the DE there is also the possibility of capturing the moments "behind the scenes" in contact with people, groups, and institutions that populate and inhabit the world that is "traveled". In some sense, both DE and all the devices addressed in this book trigger multimethod strategies where video submissions, access to YouTube, appointments on various platforms, and personal online dialogues are articulated, recreating the interview conditions beyond how controversial this may be.

It is precisely this multi-method possibility that empowers DE as a device to capture sensibilities through the multiple options of producing, receiving, recording, and emitting sensations and the emotions associated with them in connection with the world that all participants "visit", inhabit, and/or produce.

A virtual/mobile/digital world is a great factory of sensations and people related to that world are moved, indifferent, and engaged in the same way as in their "offline past". In this context, observant and observed, native and immigrant, in one post-intersectional disposition coexist beyond their genders, ages, classes, ethnicities, and any trait of perceived identity.

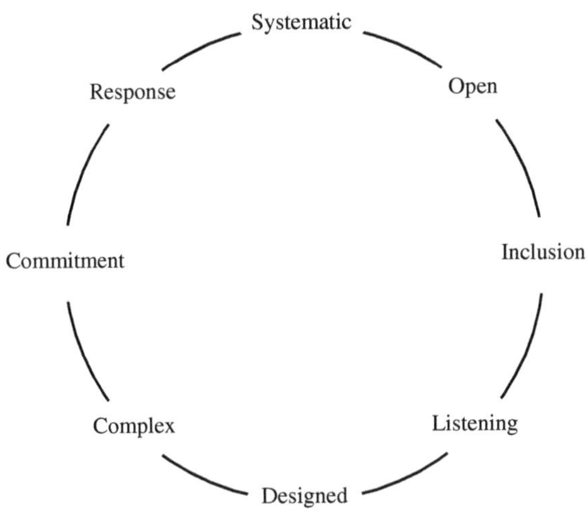


Another feature of DE is the *multidimensionality* of what is perceived/registered/interpreted, given that more and more senses are being put into play and there are more and more diverse ways of "presentifying" the non-human persons of the virtual/mobile/digital world. In this context, all DE has photos, texts, videos, songs, memes, stickers, testimonies of people, documents of companies, social movements, and various types of states. Identifying, selecting, organizing, and classifying this multiplicity of dimensions is an essential task for DE. According to the support of the selected collective or personal action, the specific weight of the dimensions varies; in this sense, DE through Instagram is different from one made through WhatsApp or the one that focuses on Facebook.

On the other hand, this multidimensionality implies diverse forms of recording, varied recording modalities, and different observation/interpretation processes. In these states of observation, there is a clear appearance of the dialectic between observing and recording, which is gradually structuring understanding. In the direction indicated, it is also necessary to underline how DE is a multi-method modality par excellence where it is possible to apply surveys, carry out interviews, participate in discussion forums, and apply some or all of the devices presented in this book.

Finally, and in direct connection with the objectives of this book, a DE captures sensibilities by constituting itself as a process that captures a "natural" moment/surface of expressiveness anchored in the virtual/mobile/digital world that is observed. What the observer sees/hears is an expressive proposal that seeks to express the motivations, ideas, and emotions of the group or person who builds that virtual/mobile/digital world. Sculptures, paintings, performances, home videos, TikTok, reels, stories, and states are some of the vehicles of creativity/expressiveness.

A practice of digital observation implies a practice of feeling where looking results in a painting of the action of the observed world. DE is a "framed" view, it is a viewer with an organization of what is seen or not seen; it is a trigger of sensations, an observer in conditions of digitality "taking it for granted", and performs reflexive monitoring of the action (*sensu* Giddens).

On the other hand, DE implies the recognition but also the elaboration of a painting of the world and the state of feeling of both those who make the observed world and those who observe it. This is what you see on the screen of the used device. Thus, a geometry of the person appears (Scribano, 2021) and tension between contexts, scenarios, and virtual/mobile/digital environments is captured in DE: texts, narratives, and material conditions of life, to which are added the infrastructure of the digital action (type of application, programming, etc.) and the forms of production of familiarity/identification.

DE must be attentive to the action's landscape, the painting of the world, and state of feeling, and the "aesthetic on the street" that involves the observed world. The expressive resources are anchored in criteria and aesthetic valuations of materials, production, and artistic sense, which are dependent on a particular historical context. However, for the expressive resources of collective actions and social protests, there is a making visible and perceptible what was previously invisible and inaudible.

Aesthetics becomes a politics of the senses, heterodox, and an opener of worlds that become palpable in (and through) that same practice. These expressive resources are linked politically, and it is usually the task of the institutional policy to silence and sterilize the "here and now" of claims and demands, transforming them into elements of their policies. "Aesthetic in the streets" then, is a way of jumping the barrier of the duplication of the natural as one of the axes of domination and "transcending" against the given.

These discussions took shape between inquiries, misinformation, and re-appropriations that could be questioned in a new scenario. Thus, in a monochromatic society where the capitalist system elaborates a set of politics for the regulation of sensations, it is very important to recover those readings where the aesthetic is linked to the possibility of configuring, showing, and activating new sensibilities. The connections between expressive resources, aesthetic-on-the-streets, and collective action will allow us to dive into the aforementioned readings.

Expressive resources offer a double possibility for reading: they are constructed and used as products of the senses (results) and are at the same time senses-in-production (inputs). From the perspective of inputs, resources are selected and used to reframe their original position in a plot of new significance, while from the perspective of results, resources are sifted through a process of meaningful production, becoming thus a "novel" utilization.

This quality of products in senses and sensibilities-in-production is what gives mobility to reading, understanding those that could have re-meaning and those that persist and are being built. So then, they are results and inputs that allow an entryway to observe legacies, reconstructions, and new creations within the practices of the action, and the senses that the subjects give to the protest, visualizing problematic areas within the conflicting networks on which the action is built.

In this context, it is possible to better understand how DE is an inquiry strategy that allows capturing sensibilities, experiencing a set of emotional ecologies, and an instrument for sharing sensations.

## References

Al-Saggaf, Y., & Williamson, K. (2004). Online communities in Saudi Arabia: Evaluating the impact on culture through online semi-structured interviews. *Forum: Qualitative Social Research*, *5*(3), 1–20.

Artero, J. P. (2010). Online video business models: YouTube vs Hulu. *Palabra Clave*, *13*(1), 111–123.

Bañuelos, J. (2009). YouTube como plataforma de la sociedad del espectáculo. *Razón y Palabra*, *14*(66), 1–26.

Beer, D., & Burrows, R. (2007). Sociology and, of and in Web 2.0: Some initial considerations. *Sociological Research Online*, *12*(5), 67–79.

Berlanga, I., & Martínez, E. (2010). Ciberlenguaje y principios de retórica clásica. Redes sociales: el caso Facebook. *Enl@ce Revista Venezolana de Información, Tecnología y Conocimiento*, 7(2), 47–61.

Bernal, P. (2013). The fallout from the McAlpine saga threatens the role of Twitter in public life. *British Politics and Policy at LSE*, February 30. http://eprints.lse.ac.uk/48535/.

Birkbak, A., Madsen, A. K., & Munk, A. K. (2021). Digital methods contributions to citizen hearings: A techno-anthropological approach to twitter and technology assessment. In Botin, L., & Børsen, T. (Eds.), *Technology Assessment in Techno-Anthropological Perspective* (pp. 105–126). Aalborg Universitetsforlag.

Botin, L., & Børsen, T. H. (Eds.) (2021). *Technology Assessment in Techno-Anthropological Perspective*. Aalborg Universitetsforlag.

Briceño Alcaraz, G. (2001). El cuerpo como performance en la sociedad del espectáculo. *Estudios sobre las Culturas Contemporáneas*, *17*(34), 9–30.

Bryson, A., Gomez, R., & Willman, P. (2010). Online social networking and trade union membership: What the Facebook phenomenon truly means for labor organizers. *Labor History*, *51*(1), 41–53.

Castillo-Torres, D., Núñez-Pacheco, R., & López-Pérez, B. E. (2019). Aportes metodológicos de la etnografía digital latinoamericana basados en Word of Warcraft.

*Revista Uruguaya de Antropología y Etnografía, 4*(1), 11–23. https://doi.org/10.29112/ruae.v4.n1.2

Chenail, R. J. (2011a). Qualitative researchers in the blogosphere: Using blogs as diaries and data. *The Qualitative Report, 16*(1), 249–254.

Chenail, R. J. (2011b). YouTube as a qualitative research asset: Reviewing user-generated videos as learning resources. *The Qualitative Report, 16*(1), 229–235.

Csordas, T. J., ed. 1994. *Embodiment and Experience: The Existential Ground of Culture and Self.* Cambridge University Press.

De Sena, A. (2011). *Colores y formas: hacia una metodología para la indagación de Internet. Sociología y publicidad en la Web.* Editorial Académico Española.

Díaz Arias, R. (2009). El vídeo en el ciberespacio: usos y lenguaje. *Comunicar, 17*(33), 63–71.

Domínguez Figaredo, D. (2007). "Sobre la intención de la etnografía virtual. *Teoría de la Educación. Educación y Cultura en la Sociedad de la Informática, 8*(1), 42–63.

Domínguez Figaredo, D., Beaulieu, A., Estalella, A., Gómez, E., Schnettler, B., & Read, R. (2007). Virtual Ethnography. *Forum: Qualitative Social Research, 8*(3), 3–7.

Fenge, L. A., Hodges, C., & Cutts, W. (2011). Seen but seldom heard: Creative participatory methods in a study of youth and risk. *International Journal of Qualitative Methods, 10*(4), 418–430.

Flam, H. (2004). Anger in repressive regimes: A footnote to domination and the arts of resistance by James Scott. *European Journal of Social Theory, 7*(2), 171–188.

Gau, L.-S., & James, K. D. (2013). "A ten-value-type framework associated with spectator sports: A qualitative inquiry." *SAGE Open, 3*(2), 1–13.

Ghosh B. (2020, December 20). Digital ethnography during the Covid-19 pandemic. *Doing Sociology.* Retrieved from https://doingsociology2020.blogspot.com/2020/12/digital-ethnography-during-covid-19.html

Halwani, R. (2010). *Philosophy of Love, Sex, and Marriage: An Introduction* (2nd ed.). Routledge.

Hine, C. (2004). *Etnografía virtual. Colección Nuevas Tecnologías y Sociedad.* Editorial UOC.

Hine, C. (2015). *Ethnography for the Internet: Embedded, Embodied and Everyday.* Routledge. https://www.doi.org/10.4324/9781003085348

Huberman, B. A., Romero, D. M., & Wu, F. (2008). Social networks that matter: Twitter under the microscope. *SSRN Working Papers Series.* Retrieved from http://dx.doi.org/10.2139/ssrn.1313405

Inglis, T. (2013). *Love.* Routledge.

Ingold, T. (2000). *The Perception of the Environment: Essays on Livelihood, Dwelling and Skill.* Routledge.

Jasper, J. M. (2011). Emotions and social movements: Twenty years of theory and research. *Annual Review of Sociology, 37*, 285–303.

Kellner, D. (2002). Presidential politics: The movie. *American Behavioral Scientist, 46*(4), 467–486.

Kozinets, R. (2021). Netnography: Seeking understanding in a networked communication society. In Quan-Haase, A., & Sloan, L. (eds.), *The SAGE Handbook of Social Media Research Methods.* SAGE.

LaBanca, F. (2011). Online dynamic asynchronous audit strategy for reflexivity in the qualitative paradigm. *The Qualitative Report, 16*(4), 1160–1171.

Lamy, L. (2016). Beyond emotion: Love as an encounter of myth and drive. *Emotion Review, 8*(2), 97–107.

Langman, L. (2002). Suppose they gave a culture war and no one came: Zippergate and the carnivalization of politics. *American Behavioral Scientist, 46*(4), 501–534.

Leon, L. (2018). Niños YouTubers y el proceso de creación de videos: evidencia de competencias transmedia en acción. *Comunicación y sociedad, 33*, 115–137. https://doi.org/10.32870/cys.v0i33.7080

Lodi, M. E., & Scanio, P. (2021). Bitácora cyborg: un recorrido por el campo de la antropología digital desde argentina. *Papeles de trabajo - Centro de Estudios Interdisciplinarios en Etnolingüística y Antropología Socio-Cultural, 42*, 112–143.

Lupton, D. (2015). *Digital Sociology*. Routledge.

Magid, R. & Schulz, L. (2017). Moral alchemy: How love changes norms. *Cognition, 167*, 135–150.

Malinowska, A., & Gratzke, M. (eds.) (2018). *The Materiality of Love: Essays on Affection and Cultural Practice*. Routledge.

Markham, A. (2020). *Doing Digital Ethnography in the Digital Age*. https://doi.org/10.31235/osf.io/hqm4g

Mera, C., & Therón, R. (2009). ViRe- YouTube: Visualizando los resultados de búsquedas en YouTube. *Avances en Sistemas e Informática, 6*(1), 135–144.

Moshe, M., & Amir, R. (2003). The sacrifice of the sons: Framing a media pseudo-event. *Jewish Political Studies Review, 15*(1–2), 155–176.

Mosquera, M. A. (2008). De la Etnografía antropológica a la Etnografía virtual. *Fermentum, 18*(53), 532–549.

Murphy, E. (2022). *An Introduction to Mobile Ethnography*. Ideemmo.

Papacharissi, Z. (2009). The virtual geographies of social networks: A comparative analysis of Facebook, LinkedIn and AsmallWorld. *New Media & Society, 11*(1–2), 199–220.

Pellegrini, A. (2016). Love objects beyond measure: Experiments in wild invention. *Psychoanalytic Psychology, 33*(1), 186–197.

Pérez Rufí, J. P., & Gómez Pérez, F. J. (2010). Paradigmas de la producción audiovisual en la Web 2.0. *Razón y Palabra, 15*(72), 0–15.

Pink, S., Horst, H., Postill, J., Hjorth, L., Lewis, T. and Tacchi, J. (2016). Introduction. In *Digital Ethnography: Principles and Practice*. Sage.

Piscitelli, A. (2009). Facebook. Esa reiterada tensión entre la sobrepromesa y la invención de nuevos mundos. *Cultura digital y prácticas creativas en educación, 6*(1), 43–52.

Pratesi, A. (2017). *Doing Care, Doing Citizenship: Towards a Micro-situated and Emotion-based Model of Social Inclusion*. Palgrave Macmillan.

Pulcini, E. (2017). What emotions motivate care? *Emotion Review, 9*(1), 64–71.

Reilly, P. (2011). The internet never forgets: Government measures to protect privacy are unlikely to succeed in the social media age. *British Politics and Policy at LSE*, July 13. Retrieved from http://eprints.lse.ac.uk/38048/.

Riem, M., Van Ijzendoorn, M., De Carli, P., Vingerhoets, A., & Bakermans-Kranenburg, M. (2017). Behavioral and neural responses to infant and adult tears: The impact of maternal love withdrawal. *Emotion, 17*(6), 1021–1029.

Roberts, D. (2003). Towards a genealogy and typology of spectacle: Some comments on debord. *Thesis Eleven, 75*(1), 54–68.

Sandberg, M., & Rossi, L. (2021). *Research Methodologies and Ethical Challenges in Digital Migration Studies: Caring for (Big) Data*. Palgrave Macmillan.

Sciara, S., & Pantaleo, G. (2018). Relationships at risk: How the perceived risk of ending a romantic relationship influences the intensity of romantic affect and relationship commitment. *Motivation and Emotion, 42*, 137–148.

Scribano, A. (2021). *Colonization of Inner Planet. 21st Century Social Theory from the Politics of Sensibilities*. Routledge.

Seebach, S. (2017). *Love and Society: Special Social Forms and the Master Emotion*. Routledge.

Skågeby, J. (2010). Online ethnographic methods: Towards a qualitative understanding of virtual community practices. In D. Ben Kei, (Ed.), *Handbook of Research on Methods and Techniques for Studying Virtual Communities: Paradigms and Phenomena*, (pp. 410–428). IGI Global.

Sloan, L., & Quan-Haase, A. (eds). (2017). *Sage Handbook of Social Media Research Methods*. Sage.

Steers, M., Øverup, C., Brunson, J., & Acitelli, L. (2016). Love online: How relationship awareness on facebook relates to relationship quality among college students. *Psychology of Popular Media Culture*, *5*(3), 203–216.

Williams, J. P. (2009). Community, frame of reference and boundary: Three sociological concepts and their relevance for virtual worlds research. *Qualitative Sociology Review*, *5*(2), 3–15.

# 5

# DRONES

## A New Way to Observe the Sensibilities of Social Interactions?

### Introduction

If we follow the intuitions of Herbert Marshall McLuhan about technologies as extensions of the human senses, the drone establishes a manipulated and controlled extension over space, modifying the experiences of time-space, and the place of the human being in it. Drones are eyes that fly, and as some distant meaning of the word in English explains, they make a buzz that is sometimes almost imperceptible. In the squares, in the stadiums, and on the roads, you can see people manipulating various forms of drones from joysticks and watching using cell phones, tablets, or other devices to see exactly what the drone is seeing.

Looking from above, looking from above without climbing, or flying are recent widespread activities of human beings. Drones are changing the possibilities of our way of seeing, looking, and observing.

We will not discuss in this work the uses of drones to monitor and punish, which have been used for some time. We intend to introduce ourselves to two features of the practices of looking on which the existence of drones has a direct impact: a) in the social practices associated with their uses, and b) as vehicles for social research.

To achieve this objective, we have divided our exposition as follows: after the presentation, a) we made explicit the connections between Society 4.0 and drones, b) we summarize the various possibilities of the use of drones, c) we introduce some key aspects of the use of drones in social research, d) we present a concrete example of research that uses drones, and finally e) we open new analysis suggestions on the potential of the use of drones in social research.

The chapter aims to show the complexity involved in the use of drones and their ability to make possible a shared and plural look from a position usually associated with power but that can be redefined as use by the social sciences as a

DOI: 10.4324/9781003319771-6

vehicle of inquiry and criticism. The work ends by suggesting that we systematically think, once again, about the transformations of the experiences of the near and the distant as central experiences of the 21st century.

## 5.1 Society 4.0 and Drones

To understand the place of drones in social practices and especially in social research, they must be included in what has been called the digital age, Revolution 4.0, Industry 4.0, and/or Society 4.0. Together with robotics, nanotechnology, and other phenomena, the unmanned movement of devices to capture and process information is one of the contemporary innovations. Drones through their impact on what will be considered "as seen" are installed in one of the most controversial edges of the construction of society in this century: the truth.

One of the most important aspects of the advent of Society 4.0 is the vertiginous development of social networks and the enormous growth of their commodification and commercial value. In this framework, the interactions between the face-to-face social world, the virtual world, and the "mobile" world of cell phones and tablets have grown exponentially. As Simply Measured maintains in its 2017 report:

> Social media spending is expected to rise to 17.3 billion by 2019 (Statista). The allocation of funds to marketing analytics is expected to see a massive increase within the next few years, according to the CMO Survey. In 2017, marketing analytics consumed just 4.6% of marketing budgets. This number could jump to almost 22% by 2020.
>
> *(Simply Measured, 2017, p. 12)*

In this context Scott Fallon (VP of Marketing, Simply Measured) maintains that:

> The expected rise in social media budgets is based on bringing social more fully into the marketing mix. Today, too many companies view social media as a siloed activity. That view is dying. Social will get more budget as more companies realize that social signals have to be attended to during the customer lifecycle. Social activity has been too long ignored from an attribution standpoint. Social channels will soon be sales channels.
>
> *(Simply Measured, 2017, p. 12)*

The consultancy firm McKinsey defines Industry 4.0 as a new step in the digitization of the manufacturing sector, driven by four clusters: more data managed by industrial companies, powerful and cheap computers, analytical capacity, and improvements in the interactions between people and machines, robots, and 3D printers. According to them, cost reduction, improvements in production lines, and the use of new databases are some of the main results of such characteristics.

Drones as instruments to see things happening "stretch" the current paradigm of sensibility by playing the role of reproducing witnesses of reality from a distance.

## 5.2 Drones: An Approach to Their Uses

In toy stores, duty free shops, and electronics stores, there is an object that until a few years ago was only available for specialized purposes: the drone. Its kinship with remote control airplanes does not make it so strange and allows us to understand that it is a remotely manned object.

If we consider a dictionary definition, this can facilitate understanding:

1. In the Dictionary of the Royal Academy it is stated: "Drone. from English drone. 1m unmanned aircraft" (Spanish Royal Academy, 2022).
2. In Linguee the translation of drone from English is the following: "drone noun (plural: drones) drone m. less frequent: drone m · drone m · unmanned aerial vehicle m · unmanned aircraft f · drone m drone verb buzz v" (Linguee, 2022).

The drone is a device that can fly without having a pilot and is therefore commanded from a distance. This device involves systems for receiving and transmitting images and data remotely.

For many, drones are a new phenomenon, but in warfare and surveillance drones are already more than a century old:

> The use of UAVs [(unmanned aerial vehicles)] in armed conflict dates back to the end of the 19th century when the first aerial → military reconnaissance photos were taken in the Spanish American War. While several systems were tested until World War II by various countries, they were of limited military use.
>
> *(Wagner, 2015, p. 6)*

For many, the use of drones is said to have a direct commercial impact in people's daily lives, as Rao et al. maintain:

> "The use of drones or unmanned aerial vehicles (UAV in English) in commercial applications has the potential to drastically alter various industries, and, in the process, change our attitudes and behaviors regarding its impact on our daily lives" (2016, p. 83).

Within the framework of the history of the use of drones, Girish Agarwal writes:

> The true inventor of a radio-controlled unmanned aircraft that could fly beyond the visual line of sight (BVLOS) of the operator, it is said, was

> Edward M. Sorensen. His invention was the first to inform an individual at a ground terminal what the airplane was doing, such as climbing, altitude, direction, RPM, and other instrumentation.
>
> *(Agarwal, 2021, p. 10)*

It is precisely this "power" of seeing beyond the line of sight that transforms these unmanned aerial devices into one of the most used and complex objects of today's digital life.

Beyond the well-known military properties and their association with war, violence, surveillance, and policing (Rivera López, 2017; Carmelini et al., 2021), drones are used for a variety of social practices.

In the literature, there are also works on the impact of drones on the physical environment, including the exposure of actions of people and socio-environmental aspects. One of the common uses of drones is monitoring traffic congestion (Kellermann et al., 2020).

Drones are also being used in research and artistic production. Leote and Cavalhieri (2019) attest to the creative processes that gave rise to the first techno performance with a drone, held at the International and Interinstitutional Research Group on Convergence between Art, Science and Technology (GIIP).

There is also a set of works that ask about the challenges, promises, and risks of using drones to identify, systematize, and solve social problems in particularly complex regions of the planet such as the research on Africa by Nicki Washington, which in its conclusion states:

> As the non-military use of drones continues to increase, countries and governments are exploring the applications of the technology to solve critical problems in a number of areas. However, countries in Africa have led the successful implementation of drones to provide socially relevant solutions to problems that span a wide range of areas. Given less stringent regulations and more government partnerships with leading drone development companies (including designating testing areas for drone research).
>
> *(Washington, 2018, p. 11)*

There are inquiries about the social uses of drones; an example in the context of social analysis was conducted by Mohamed et al. (2020), who pointed out the use of drones in smart cities. It is also possible to identify a field of analysis on the environmental impacts of drones used to deliver products from online shopping systems, such as the research by Koiwanit (2018).

As can be seen, the social, commercial, and scientific importance of drones goes beyond the mere use of warfare or security. But also, according to Serafinelli, it brings with it demands and criticisms of an ethical/political nature:

> Drones are an increasingly important social phenomenon. They are widely understood as unstaffed aircraft, generally fitted with cameras that can be

> remotely controlled and used for recreational and commercial purposes Alongside professional uses, the drone market found fertile ground with civilian fliers who show particular enthusiasm in the new visual opportunities they afford. In fact, they engage with viewing and capturing innovative visual content. Besides the interest in new visual perspectives, the widespread use of drones amongst civilians generates concern in relation to personal privacy, ethics, safety and security.
>
> *(Serafinelli, 2022, p. 1)*

In the horizon of what has been outlined, the use of drones modifies the connection between seeing, looking, and observing and thereby brings these practices of use closer to social research. Drones as observation and recording devices have long been incorporated into social research:

> Drones, as prime examples of IOT engagements, combine physical and digital technologies and can produce large amounts of data. The challenge lies in the social arrangements adopted for processing this information, not simply its production, in research and other fields. The boundaries between research and application become less clear with this and other digital innovations. Drones as a technology are not a paradigm shift, but they could evolve into people transportation and other forms. In combination with other actual-measuring-and-acting devices, they help shift research foci and social research capabilities.
>
> *(Burns, 2016, p. 1)*

Within the framework of that pointed out by Burns, it is possible to emphasize both the fact that drones are part of the transformations of Society 4.0 and that in them the body of the researcher is articulated with technology. On the one hand, drones make it clear that when societies change, social research is modified, and, on the other hand, even in the case of "increased technification" in observation, the body/emotion of the researcher remains of vital importance.

Although, as indicated in the text of Hall and Wahab, there are today unfulfilled "promises" made by drone technology regarding its use in social sciences, and without a doubt, it can be seen how, according to these same authors in the fields of geography, archaeology, and ecology, the incorporation of drones is challenging:

> The application of drones in the social sciences as data collection tools comes on the back of the use of satellite imagery in the same endeavours. The latter can be traced to the mid-1990s when the National Aeronautics and Space Administration (NASA) approached the research community to realize the potential of satellite imagery to specifically address questions which social scientists are preoccupied with. Notwithstanding the high expectations from this collaboration expressed in People and Pixels:

> Linking Remote Sensing and Social Science (Livermore et al., 1998), the results have been meagre, and their added value questioned. Much of the difficulties that limited the success of using remotely sensed satellite imagery – coarse resolution of most readily available datasets, the challenge with cloud cover, particularly in the tropics, and limitations relating to temporal resolutions – persist till date.
>
> *(Hall & Wahab, 2021, p. 3)*

This gives us another element that becomes important in the framework of this chapter: drones incorporate the multidimensionality of space as a "new" aspect of doing social research.

> We proffer the Nephosphere as a loosely-defined class G airspace of expanding participation, encompassing the otherwise inaccessible volume that exists above the gravity-defined bounds of human habitation but below strictly defined flight zones, analogous in some ways to the open sea. The Nephosphere is a space previously only experienced from relatively static aerial positions such as balloons and kites, or through architectural vantage points like rooftops. So, although the Nephosphere has played a prominent role in the human imagination, the drone is an agile means with which we can access the Nephosphere, rendering the volume of increasing political importance. Yet geographical scholarship of the drone to date has framed such methodologies along dichotomous lines that are, we suggest, somewhat blinkered to the potentials and complexities of the technology. "Like satellites before them, drones have moved beyond their military uses to reshape our vertical publics" (McCosker, 2015, p. 2) and we thus follow Noys' (2015, p. 14) suggestion that "reading the vertical as a site of pure domination underestimates the complexity and tension in constituting the vertical as a site of power". An expanded sense of drone methodologies in geography, both critical and astute, will shape imaginations and practices.
>
> *(Garrett & Anderson, 2018, p. 4)*

As Garrett and Anderson (2018) express it, the use of drones involves the paradoxical situation that social research has always had: being situated on the edge between domination and insubordination.

Beyond violence, surveillance, and punishment, the daily use of drones opens critical horizons regarding various aspects of social interaction; in this sense, Ramírez López (2015) has analyzed the drone impact on the right to privacy.

This brief tour of the "uses" of drones, and the variety and intensity of actions carried out by and from these devices allow us to build a clearer scenario for their use in the methodology of social research.

From a perspective close to that, here mention "Nexus", the Newsletter of the Australian Association of Sociology, where Edgar Burns of La Trobe University expounded on drones in the context of the Internet of Things (IoT):

> Social research intersects each milieu noted above. A new option for studying group processes sounds mundane and useful. Drones also invoke new ethical questions, the answers to which will evolve to meet the new 'normal' and other digital circumstances that extend each scenario. This will occur in combination with other digital IOT capabilities. The corny image of the annoying neighbor with a drone is actually important because it raises most of these potential ethical issues: personal privacy, civil rights, nuisance, theft, harm, harassment, informed consent. It may be that ambivalence is an appropriate stance regarding drones, as for other innovative technologies (Matthewman, 2011). Consider this: drones are equally adept at delivering life-saving medical drugs and extending the scourge of ice addiction and supply. This is consistent with Manion and Goodrum's (2000, p. 18) broader observation that the internet releases two opposing possibilities, one towards emancipation and one towards domination.
>
> *(Burns, 2016)*

Another of the central aspects of the widespread nature of drones is what Artega Botello calls the "politics of verticality", playing with the drone's gaze from above and the imposition from above by the state in the systematic surveillance of drones' citizens:

> As in other places, the borders in Latin America are now more porous and elastic, deep and flexible, which allows the so-called border lines to end up becoming strips of greater thickness. The population flows that pass through them are made up of diverse groups and individuals of illegal workers, traffickers of merchandise, drugs and human beings, as well as other "subversives" or "terrorists". The gaze of the drones provides this scenario with a visual field that captures the mobility of these actors in large territories, where they can be coupled or merged into a single region.
>
> *(Arteaga Botello, 2016, p. 280)*

The use of drones could not (yet?) be classified as omnipresent, even less if one thinks of underdeveloped countries, but there is certainly a tendency to extend their use. In this context, the uses and "new" social practices of drones seem to have an impact on social life, the modes of interaction, and the practices of feeling.

Firstly, it is possible to maintain that use of drones should be differentiated from its property. Secondly, some categories of use can be established according to the possible uses of the drone's technical capabilities: taking photos, making films, sending geo-referenced data, transporting objects, etc. Thirdly, the objectives of the aforementioned technological uses are entertainment, work, production, communication, security, etc. Fourth, accessing a drone, like any technological device, can be said to be acquiring a status symbol, an opportunity to earn income, or differentiated and distinctive socialization spaces.

1) It is not necessary to buy a drone to use one. Some people and companies provide the device, the pilot, and the "editing" of what has been captured in exchange for a price that has already begun to "standardize" in the market. Producers of the film "Your Adventure", photographers of weddings, baptisms, birthdays of all classes and all religions, and geo-referenced data production agencies are some of the vehicles to use without having to buy a drone.

   There are multiple options for what to do with a drone and how to own one: from those used as toys for children and adolescents that, connected to their cell phones, extend the possibilities of expanding their digitalization of the world, to those that accompany their owners in their hobbies (mountain bike, climbing, hang gliding, etc.), to those who acquire a drone to set up a business.
2) Drones take photos from positions from which a human being cannot, they film scenes that are tied to the flow of everyday life in a way that an observer cannot, they can capture a complex set of data, organize and reference them geographically and positionally, and also, among others, can carry objects and make them accessible in situations and spaces that are difficult for a person to access. All these qualities make drones new social actors managed remotely and thereby modifying the ecology of the social practices that involve them.
3) "To make see is to make feel" seems to be the dictum of everyday life in the 21st century. With Instagram, Snapchat, and/or WhatsApp, the "custom of showing" has become mass and globalized. From entertainment to surveillance, today drones can create snapshots of the here and now. Whether to produce, communicate, and/or enjoy, drones transport qualities of flying to the subjects: the experience of a (third?) dimension – whether that experience is for its own sake, to sell the recreation of an imagined experience, or to guarantee maximum observability.
4) Using/buying a drone gives the acquirer a different status given that drones are not omnipresent and having one gives an impression of exclusivity and prestige. In the same way, a set of expectations and fantasies are created that are situated in a wide space marked by desires. But as has also been insinuated, the "drone market" is a prosperous and growing business not only in the use of drones but also in the production of devices, software, and hardware for them, repairs, among other areas. In addition, piloting courses, credential exams, fan clubs, websites and/or Facebook, meetings, conferences of experts and lay people constitute new and attractive spaces for socialization in societies where novelty characterizes social networks and everyday life.

## 5.3 Drones and Social Research

The use of drones in warfare has given rise to a myriad of works in research in defence, geopolitics, and international law (Wagner, 2015; Schwarz, 2016).

Philosophical theories on drones have also been developed, such as that of Chamayou who explicitly explains his intentions as follows:

> The intention of this book is to subject the drone to a philosophical investigation. In this matter, I follow the precept expressed by Canguilhem: "Philosophy is a reflection for which all foreign material is good and, we would gladly say, in which all good material must be foreign." If the drone lends itself in particular to this kind of approach, it is because it is an "unidentified violent object": as soon as one tries to think about it in terms of established categories, intense confusion arises around notions as elementary as zones or places (geographical and ontological categories), virtue or bravery (ethical categories), warfare or conflict (categories at once strategic and legal-political). I should first like to explain these crises of intelligibility by bringing to light the contradictions they express. At the root of them all lies the elimination, already rampant but here absolutely radicalized, of any immediate relation of reciprocity.
>
> *(Chamayou, 2015, p. 14)*

From a different perspective, the humanitarian possibilities of drones have been addressed:

> In recent years, the humanitarian cost of drone wars has become the focus of international attention. Much less visibly, terms such as humanitarian drones, drone humanitarianism, drones for human rights and humanitarian missiles have been migrating from the far corners of the blogosphere into mainstream discussions of humanitarian action and humanitarian policy. As the "humanitarian drone" gains currency as a political concept, it is important to disentangle the ideas from which that concept has emerged and to think about the implications for humanitarian action. In this article, we do so by considering a range of actual and projected transfers of unmanned aerial vehicles (UAVs, hereinafter also drones) from the global battlefield to the humanitarian emergency zone.
>
> *(Sandvik & Lohne, 2014, p. 2)*

It is also observable how from geography, ecology, and agriculture, among other fields, many scientific disciplines are considering the potential of drones both in research and teaching:

> "There is already a range of academic uses that go beyond mere military engagement in non-social science settings: UAVs are used in geology, environmental science and archaeological geophysics for aerial data capture in topographical, geological, architectural and infrastructural surveys" (Birtchnell & Gibson, 2015, p. 183).

This chapter aims to extract some guidelines to create an approach to the use of drones in social research. However, before that let us synthesize some of the possible connections between the digital world and social research.

From the last decade of the last century, studies on what was happening on the Internet, what was beginning to happen in the virtual world, and how this gave rise to new styles and sources of research multiplied: the construction of the "personalities on-line" (Paap & Raybeck, 2005), on the "architectures" of interaction in the nascent social networks (Papacharissi, 2009), and on the characteristics of the new phenomena that were appearing in the world of globalized communication (Mollett et al., 2011).

We have already conducted a set of reflections on the use of WhatsApp (Scribano, 2017a) and Instagram (Scribano, 2017b) that link digitalization, Society 4.0, and the surface of social research where the analysis that follows should be added.

To concretize the possible uses of drones in social research, we can perform a triple approach: a) according to technological possibilities, b) according to the "above, transverse, and in motion (ATM) effect", and c) concerning the relations between seeing, looking, and observing.

A first approximation takes us, on the one hand, directly to the technological capabilities of drones to record social scenes, individual and collective practices, and on the other, to the data storage and management capacity of this device. The photos, the films, and the georeferencing capacity modify not only the volume of what is possible to record but also the quality. Some of the qualitative characteristics are: multidimensionality, possibilities of 360° vision, and recursivity of the register. The various positionalities of the vehicle allow the identification of individuals, groups, and social collectives, as well as "following" the movements of the actors in the place of action. These capacities are complemented by the possibility of simultaneously programming the processes of observation, registration, and systematization and storage of information.

A second approach to the powers of the drone as an observation device is what we are going to call "ATM effect" (above, transverse and moving). The device enables a dimensional anchoring by which the researcher is in a different plane than his observation instrument, which is in the air – a perspective fixing, since the device allows the user to observe the front/back of the scene and ensures the view from all angles, since the drone can move in the observed scene with more observation points than the researcher.

From above, from a height, a transverse and diagonal view while in motion is a novel way to capture sensibilities. ATM is a sensation that produces sensations as an interpretation of the digitized real. In the folds of Society 4.0, the transformation emerges of an arm into a mechanism for seeing human beings in different ways.

ATM is a dialectic that transforms social inquiry as an unwanted effect of the action of the surveillance and punishment systems and becomes a vehicle for criticism.

The ATM effect is based on the potential of a technology that expands the observation possibilities of the researcher and challenges us to consider the edges between seeing, looking, and observing, which brings us to the third approach.

The use of drones allows enhancing an exemplary circle between observation, recording, and interpretation, because at the moment it is seen it is also observed, and at the same time it creates a look on a social fact. Looking may not only be a motivation of those in command of the device but may also be a bridge to a participatory view that transforms into community observation.

## 5.4 Doing Research with Drones

Below is the experience carried out and coordinated by Pedro Lisdero, associate researcher of CONICET in Argentina, and co-coordinator of the Study Program on Collective Action and Social Conflict of the CIECS of the National University of Cordoba.

The purpose of the synthesis presented below is to give an "example" of the use of drones in social research, emphasizing how it is more than necessary to articulate theoretical, procedural, epistemic, and ontological perspectives in such a way that the "use of the drone" not be mere filming from the air. Basically, the research carried out consists of a multi-method strategy, which includes approaches from the creative/expressive, digital "ethnography", and the recording/dialogue/interpretation of and about the zenith gaze. In addition, the proposal considers the effort to describe the images and their interpretations from three different angles: the zenith gaze, the level gaze, and the oblique gaze.

At the crossroads between visual sociology, work, and emotions, Lisdero set out to investigate some of the transformations of the world of work, particularly in this case, the experience of fairground workers in the city of Córdoba, particularly in the Espacio Caseros.

It is specifically a collective space for workers, or as they define themselves "an organization of producers in defence of arts and crafts", which brings together more than 200 individuals who hold – among other activities – a fair (rotating stalls selling goods) in a central area of the city of Córdoba.

The research is based on a set of particular features of the analyzed fair that differentiate it from similar ones in that same city: the demands of the collective of sellers put into play the very complexity of the *worker* identity in these specific social formations, features that are linked to the maintenance of the fair and the demands for visibility associated with social conflict *communicate* social processes that exceed the *problems* of this specific group and the *aesthetics* put into play in the interaction of subject and environment (in the instance of work, in the expressive relationship with *its products*, or even in the public intervention of the fair).

An essential component of this chapter regarding the experience is the articulation of the relationship with the vendors where: a) a relationship of informed consent of the investigation and an approach to their identity is first produced, b) the strategy of digital ethnography with the participation of the stallholders and a Facebook group is *opened*, c) the records are made from a multi-method perspective including from drones, and d) the images and Facebook interactions are interpreted.

Lisdero points out that a first demarcation movement about the "gaze" on his object of inquiry led him to underline three analytical features: the appropriation of urban space (which we will address here through the metaphor of "a gaze from above"), the dimensions that have to do with the configuration of the spaces, organization, and work processes (which we will understand here from the "close look"), and finally the processes of identity construction (for which we will establish the metaphor of an "oblique look").

It is in this framework that one of the most important features emerges for the purposes of this chapter: the recovery of the complementarity of the zenith, flush, and oblique gaze, which make up a particular theoretical-methodological strategy.

To better understand the device, Lisdero systematizes some assumptions of his research strategy:

> Thus, we would like to emphasize that although we support here the capacity of visual experiences to contribute to the understanding of specific phenomena, on the other hand, we believe that it is necessary remain alert about the possibilities of being trapped in "the bias of the visible as verification of the truth", "reflecting" images instead of recognizing that they are part of – they are crossed – by the sensibilities that are the object of the analysis itself.
>
> *(Lisdero, 2017, p. 77)*

It is from these assumptions that an experience of/with "the visual" is proposed, which involves four components:

1. Potentializing "what the image communicates", that is, the possibility of investigating social phenomena beyond verbal narration. Following Scribano's proposal, we are interested in "[t]he capacities to grant meanings and to multiply the social modes of observing and observing oneself that photography possesses, [and that] make it one of the most outstanding candidates when it comes to re-take the sensations" (Scribano, 2008b, p. 256).

   *(Lisdero, 2017, p. 78)*

2. Being reflexively aware of the fact that fairs and their workers have been the object of research from different disciplines and that therefore this experience is not exhaustive, and its main objective is to highlight some central features of the discussion on this object of research and the use of drones.
3. Investigate "what the image is missing", criticizing the politics of the senses as an obstacle to and knowledge of the conflict. In other words, plotting a strategy of critical knowledge towards the verification that "[t]he organic and social senses allow us to convey what seems unique and unrepeatable, such as individual sensations, and at the same time elaborate the unnoticed

work of the in-corporation of the social made emotion (Scribano, 2008b, p. 255).

*(Lisdero, 2017, p. 78)*

4. Emphasize "what the image shows", since although the appearance of the image is a captivating specular circumstance, it shows what the camera-eye wants and can see; however, this also makes it possible to account for the visible side of the subjects-in-position with respect to a landscape (Scribano, 2008b, p. 256).

*(Lisdero, 2017, p. 78)*

In this context, the strategy followed by Lisdero aims to systematically produce different types of visual information that make it possible to obtain a broader view of the object of study from its articulation in a complementary manner.

The strategy also includes the explanation of assumptions of interpretation from which a double movement distinguishable at the analytical level is pointed out. H. Becker's proposal is replicated, repeatedly observing the photographs, exhaustively describing the elements, and relating these annotations to what is known about the life of the people, the circumstances of the taking of the photograph, the reaction of the subjects, etc.

Lisdero emphasizes that Becker explains that this makes it possible to oppose some habits of superficial reading, by forcing the elements present in the image to be enunciated and inserting them into a story and relationships. The second movement, made explicit, take up the fundamentals of "photo elicitation", a strategy proposed by Harper (2002) exploring the potential of using images in conducting in-depth interviews.

The images that make up this angle of the visual experience could be recognized from Mauss's early recommendation to "take height", and consequently, recover the potential stated in the brief exploration of the intersection between social sciences and aerial photography.

In this context, Lisdero maintains:

> The warnings of De Certau (1996) about a zenithal gaze that "moves away and ignores" the vitality of an urban space lived and legible "flush" are partly provocative for our strategy. Thus, different investigations have warned that the productivity of "area photography" associates its analytical performance with the possibility of relating them to other sources of information. In this way, it is not a question here of reifying the forgetfulness of the experience of a "dead-image" that draws an opaque, blind cartography, stripped of the sensibilities of the subjects that inhabit it. But on the contrary, in the tension with the rest of the "proposed gazes", the zenith would evoke these same tensions, emphasizing a specific angle on the urban space, the practices and the self, in the tension that means a point of sight scarcely explored in everyday life.
>
> *(Lisdero, 2017, p. 78)*

In this framework, it is possible to understand how the images produced in the context of this *zenith gaze* were elaborated from aerial shots made with an unmanned aerial vehicle (UAV). Due to the characteristics of the image obtained in Lisdero's research, as well as the angle of the shot made, the image is more suitable for geo-referencing, and therefore, for relating to other aerial images of greater scope, such as images extracted from Google Earth, allowing in turn to expand the analytical range implied by spatial information. On the other hand, other shots at 60 metres and 20 metres make it possible to visualize in more detail the relationships of the subjects with each other, the proximities and distances between workers and passers-by, and other urban spaces, from a different perspective. To *validate* and *evaluate* the relationship between the gaze captured and the height of the image made, a process of production sought to vary the altitude of the shot: a first image was taken at a higher altitude (110 metres), which allowed expanding the visual range of the urban site of the fair, making a greater amount of information available that will result in a more complex description of the environment.

It also allows us to see the relationships of appropriation of space through (although it was not a direct objective in this phase of the investigation) these images with a greater amount of information.

They are very useful for the application of a series of quantitative analytical tools, which allow accounting for the number of stalls at the fair, of vendors, and estimating the number of people who attend.

In this context, it is easy to understand how the use of drones as an instrument of social inquiry allows the creation and resumption of mixed and participatory strategies. The people who participate in the research can share and interpret the zenith view, which democratizes, at least in part, the politics of verticality so widespread on the planet.

With drones, eyes can literally be multiplied, and with this the assessment of social relationships in the context of increased autonomy and sharing between researchers and researched.

## 5.5 By Way of a New Opening

This vehicle of *other looks* brings into discussion the familiar plots between proximity and distance in social inquiry.

The use of drones always implies a serious ethical problem; consequently, there are numerous academic articles on the matter in different areas: the problem of control (West & Bowman, 2016), humanitarian use (Wang et al., 2021), data privacy (Finn & Wright, 2016), and journalism (Waite, 2012), among many others.

As we have already pointed out, the topic of drones brings with it discussions of political and social epistemology due to the concrete crossing of disciplines such as cybernetics, psychology, and sociology, which also imply carrying out urgent processes of theoretical reflection. In this direction Carmelini and his colleagues conclude their work by synthesizing:

> The body dronization process discussed in this work is not a recent or sudden phenomenon. In fact, the body, eye, and cognition automation and displacement dates back to the most basic longings of modern knowledge, either from the perspective of the eye, leading us to the early modern times of technology and science through perspective, map, printer, psychology, cybernetics, and cognitive sciences or from the perspective of the foot, whose substrate docks in transportation systems and urbanism.
>
> *(Carmelini et al., 2021, p. 165)*

Among the ethical problems that the use of drones for social research brings, we can highlight three: first, the reference to the privacy of the subjects, second, issues related to informed consent, and third, the problem of surveillance.

Regarding privacy, it is possible to observe three components of a discussion that remains open, which are related to each other. Firstly, *digital life*, in general, has experienced a modification of privacy where making public what is private has been normalized, and in this sense, in social research it is thought that one must pay attention to geopolitical and geocultural differences, and political sensibilities of what is designated as private in each place. Secondly, along with the previous point, the field of horizons related to the politics of privacy and the politics of lives (*sensu* Giddens) emerges. Thirdly is the complexity of the *place of the other* in the investigation, where the risks of silencing and discrimination can be perceived.

In relation to informed consent, this way of inquiry is directly related to all the platforms and applications of the digital age where the subjects voluntarily accept public exposure and consent to it. From this view, it is easier to understand why attending a march, going to a football stadium, and participating in a political meeting in the streets are practices that involve being exposed to the gaze of the other and consequently to a *partial authorization* of the publicity of the action. That authorization does not have a specific objective, but it could be said that the person who attends does so, so that others know they are attending and see it. This is clearly a controversial and complex issue, since authoritarianism, control, and persecution can arise from the same arguments.

In conjunction with above-mentioned points, the problem of monitoring the control of discipline appears across all areas, and a complex plot of domination can occur, where the social scientist must clearly discern if his practice is oriented towards listening and autonomy or if it is part of a mechanism of observation and punishment.

Being aware of these three features at least allows us to understand how the use of drones can also be carried out as a reflective practice that involves the researcher's purpose being in focus.

Among various ways of systematizing the problems and possibilities of research practice with ethical criteria carried out with drones, Anjali Singh (2019) systematizes them as follows:

> *Exempt human subjects research:* Some studies can qualify for exempt human subjects research in case: a) the information obtained cannot be linked to

> the subjects; b) disclosure of information will not harm a person's status and reputation; c) a limited committee review is required. *Non-exempt human subjects research:* Interestingly, an expedited review is also feasible in non-exempt human subjects research which imposes no more than minimal risks to human subjects. In such studies, consent can be waived or altered: a) in case there's only a minimal risk to subjects; b) waiver won't affect subjects' well-being; c) the research could not be carried out without identifiable private information or the requested waiver. Note that minimal risks refer to both drone accidents and the potential loss of confidentiality.
>
> *(Singh, 2019)*

According to the research presented in this chapter, one way of configuring an ethically safe research practice can be done by consulting the community through community organizations, or by digital or face-to-face means. Resnik and Elliott argue the following:

> However, in most cases it would still be prudent for researchers to consult with community members before the research takes place to assure them that their privacy, confidentiality, and welfare will be protected. Researchers could inform community members about proposed studies and methods used to protect privacy and confidentiality, such as redaction of personal identifiers and security measures, and give community members an opportunity to ask questions. These consultation activities could also allow community members to inform the researchers about sensitive information that might be collected and that would be important to handle with care. This is likely to be especially important in international contexts where the researchers might not understand all the cultural concerns of the communities being observed. Community consultation is not a substitute for informed consent, but it can help to establish trust and cooperation among community members and make researchers more sensitive to community concerns.
>
> *(Resnik & Elliott, 2019, p. 10)*

In close connection to the ethical problems of social research, the use of drones brings with it the need to rethink the "why" of the research. And it is in this sense that we find ourselves again with the demand/challenge of social research as a transformation of the world. The images recorded by the drone should meet three requirements: a) that they are accessible to people who have been recorded voluntarily or involuntarily, b) that access to said images be as wide as possible without breaking the privacy contract with the people observed, and finally, c) that an elaboration of the tacit or explicit limits of the drone action be provided.

## Reference list


Agarwal, G. (2021). *Droneopticon: Privacy implications of civilian drones in the EU. Civilian Drones, Visual Privacy and EU Human Rights Law.* Routledge Research in Human Rights Law.

Arteaga Botello, N. (2016). Política de la verticalidad: drones, territorio y población en América Latina. *Región y Sociedad, XXVIII*(65), 263–292. http://www.redalyc.org/articulo.oa?id=10243267008

Birtchnell, T. & Gibson, C. (2015). Less talk more drone: Social research with UAVs. *Journal of Geography in Higher Education, 39*(1), 182–189. http://dx.doi.org/10.1080/03098265.2014.1003799

Burns, E. (2016). Drones and social research nexus. *Newsletter Australian Sociological Association*. October 20. Retrieved from https://nexus.tasa.org.au/drones-and-social-research/

Carmelini, J. L., Mizoguchi, D. H., & De Araújo, P. F. M. (2021). Corpo-drone: Governamentalidade algorítmica e a modulação espaço-imagética. *Matrizes, 15*(1), 147–168. https://doi.org/10.11606/issn.1982-8160.v15i1p147-168

Chamayou, G. (2015). *A Theory of the Drone* (J. Lloyd, transl.). The New York Press.

Finn, R. L., & Wright, D. (2016). Privacy, data protection and ethics for civil drone practice: A survey of industry, regulators and civil society organisations. *Computer Law & Security Review, 32*(4), 577–586.

Garrett, B., & Anderson, K. (2018). Drone methodologies: Taking flight in human and physical geography. *Transactions of the Institute of British Geographers, 43*(3), 341–359. https://doi.org/10.1111/tran.12232

Hall, O., & Wahab, I. (2021). The use of drones in the spatial social sciences. *Drones, 5*(4), 112. https://doi.org/10.3390/drones5040112

Harper, D. (2002) Talking about pictures: A case for photo elicitation. *Visual Studies, 17*(1), 13–26. https://doi.org/10.1080/14725860220137345

Kellermann, R., Biehle, T., & Fischer, L. (2020). Drones for parcel and passenger transportation: A literature review. *Transportation Research Interdisciplinary Perspectives, 4*, 100088. https://doi.org/10.1016/j.trip.2019.100088

Koiwanit, J. (2018). Analysis of environmental impacts of drone delivery on an online shopping system. *Advances in Climate Change Research, 9*(3), 201–207. https://doi.org/10.1016/j.accre.2018.09.001

Leote, R., & Cavalhieri, C. P. (2019). Tecnoperformance e instalação: possibilidades emergentes de produção artística com drones. *ARS (São Paulo)*, 17(35), 239–256. https://doi.org/10.11606/issn.2178-0447.ars.2019.152523

Linguee. (2022). *Drone.* Retrieved from https://www.linguee.es/ingles-espanol/traduccion/drone.html

Lisdero, P. (2017). Desde las nubes... Sistematización de una estrategia teórico metodológica visual. *Revista Latinoamericana de Metodología de la Investigación Social – ReLMIS, 13*(7), 69–90.

Mohamed, N., Al-Jaroodi, J., Jawhar, I., Idries, A., & Mohammed, F. (2020). Unmanned aerial vehicles applications in future smart cities. *Technological Forecasting and Social Change, 153*, 119293. https://doi.org/10.1016/j.techfore.2018.05.004

Mollett, A., Moran, D., & Dunleavy, P. (2011). Using Twitter in university research, teaching and impact activities. In *Impact of Social Sciences: Maximizing the Impact of Academic Research*. LSE Public Policy Group, London School of Economics and Political Science. Retrieved from http://eprints.lse.ac.uk/38489/

Paap, K., & Raybeck, D. (2005). A differently gendered landscape: Gender and agency in the web-based personals. *Electronic Journal of Sociology, 9*(4), 1–44.

Papacharissi, Z. (2009). The virtual geographies of social networks: A comparative analysis of Facebook, LinkedIn and AsmallWorld. *New Media & Society, 11*(1–2), 199–220.

Ramírez López, S. (2015). Del campo de batalla a las calles: el derecho a la intimidad en la era de los drones. *Revista Derecho del Estado, 35*, 181–199.

Rao, B., Gopi, A. G., & Maione R. (2016). The societal impact of commercial drones. *Technology in Society, 45*, 83–90.

Resnik, D. B., & Elliott, K. C. (2019). Using drones to study human beings: Ethical and regulatory issues. *Science and Engineering Ethics, 25*(3), 707–718. https://doi.org/10.1007/s11948-018-0032-6

Rivera López, E. (2017). Los drones, la moralidad profunda y las convenciones de la guerra. *Isonomía. Revista de Teoría y Filosofía del Derecho, 46*, 11–28.

Sandvik, K. B., & Lohne, K. (2014). The rise of the humanitarian drone: Giving content to an emerging concept. *Millennium: Journal of International Studies, 43*(1), 145–164.

Schwarz, E. (2016). Prescription drones: On the techno-biopolitical regimes of contemporary 'ethical killing'. *Security Dialogue, 47*(1), 59–75.

Scribano, A. (2017a). Miradas cotidianas. El uso de Whatsapp como experiencia de investigación social. *Revista Latinoamericana de Metodología de la Investigación Social – ReLMIS, 13*(7), 8–22.

Scribano, A. (2017b). Instaimagen: mirar tocando para sentir. *RBSE Revista Brasileira de Sociologia da Emoção, 16*(47), 45–55.

Serafinelli, E. (2022). Imagining the social future of drones. *Convergence: The International Journal of Research into New Media Technologies*, 1–16. https://doi.org/10.1177/13548565211054904

Simply Measured. (2017). *The State of Social Marketing.* 2017 Annual Report. Retrieved from https://get.simplymeasured.com/rs/135-YGJ-288/images/SM_StateOfSocial-2017.pdf

Singh, A. (2019). *Ethics of Drone Use for Human Research. Drone Hypothesis, Drone Science.* Retrieved from https://conductscience.com/ethics-of-drone-use-for-human-research/#7

Spanish Royal Academy. (2022). *Drone.* Retrieved from http://dle.rae.es/?id=ED2QqnQ

Wagner, M. (March 24, 2015). *Unmanned Aerial Vehicles. Max Planck Encyclopedia of Public International Law.* Oxford University Press, University of Miami Legal Studies Research Paper No. 15-12.

Waite, M. (2012, October 26). How we use a drone to cover drought. *Drone Journalism Lab.* Retrieved from http://www.dronejournalismlab.org/post/34363827984/how-we-used-a-drone-to-cover-drought

Wang, N., Christen, M., & Hunt, M. (2021). Ethical Considerations Associated with "Humanitarian Drones": A Scoping Literature Review. *Science and Engineering Ethics, 27*(4), 1–21. https://doi.org/10.1007/s11948-021-00327-4

Washington, A. N. (2018). A survey of drone use for socially relevant problems: Lessons from Africa. *African Journal Of Computing & ICT, 11*(3), 1–11.

West, J. P., & Bowman, J. S. (2016). The domestic use of drones: An ethical analysis of surveillance issues. *Public Administration Review, 76*(4), 649–659.

# 6

# DIGITAL CREATIVE EXPERIENCE

## A Sensibility Capture Device

### Introduction

The COVID-19 pandemic has given us new ways of social inquiry. In the context of what we have developed since 2009 as Expressive Creative Encounters, we carry out the task of adapting this device to capture sensibilities in the virtual/mobile/digital environment.

In this context, based on the use of the photo, emojis/stickers, and drawings, we designed Digital Creative Experiences through the use of Zoom as a platform for communication, creativity, and expressiveness.

Digital Creative Experiences (DCEs) connect directly with three dimensions that, at least, should be presented schematically: a) social research based on creativity/expressiveness, b) the sociology of bodies/emotions, and c) the use of Zoom as a platform for dialogue, communication, and education. In what follows we will make a tight synthesis of these dimensions as an introduction to DCEs.

This chapter seeks to make a first presentation of a DCE carried out in six countries of Latin America with young students of sociology in a situation of confinement due to the pandemic in 2020.

To achieve the proposed objectives, the following exposition strategy has been adopted: a) the context of "birth" of DCEs as creative/expressive devices is introduced, b) some features of the use of Zoom in social research are elaborated, c) the components of DCEs are synthesized, d) some examples of DCEs' drawings are shown, and e) finally some keys to understanding the usefulness of DCEs are outlined.

DOI: 10.4324/9781003319771-7

## 6.1 Creativity/Expressiveness: A Journey to Understand the Social

The creativity of human beings is a recurring theme in the social sciences. The tight synthesis presented here is directly connected to the reflections on creativity and imagination made by Lev S. Vygotsky and Mikhail M. Bakhtin, among others (Scribano, 2011). Given the available space, it has been preferred that the most important aspects referring directly to the objectives of this book be developed, without going into further details on the data.

In the context of experiencing creativity as a power to capture and transform the world, qualitative inquiry breaks away and builds renewed paths to see the world with others and those who participate in research. The subjects, when creating, inscribe on multiple surfaces various ways of expressing their emotions and sensations. If creativity is used as a logic of inquiry, what emerges from the subjects, what is *interesting* to appear from the researcher, and what is not manifested mutually stress each other. These *findings* become a knot through which what the researcher seeks and what the subjects *do* are articulated.

Expressiveness is precisely making clear what is implied, it is un-wrapping, de-compressing. In expressiveness, the tacit (that which is taken for granted according to the mechanisms of social supportability and the regulatory regimes of sensations) manifests itself and becomes present. Expressing oneself is also a vehicle for disarming the packets of class habitus, for removing what is involved and putting it in connection with what was involved. Likewise, the expressiveness of the subjects decompresses what is *tight*, *concentrated* in the muteness of the differential and systematic appropriation of the uses of the word as the only way of saying.

The DCEs that we present here are part of a search to capture the sensations, emotions, and sensibilities *beyond* the word within the framework of an unequal distribution of speech.

DCE is also part of a set of individual and collective efforts that we have called "Expressive Creative Encounters" (Scribano, 2013), "Danced Interviews" (Scribano, 2014), "Eating Experiences" (Scribano et al., 2014), and applied an experience based on the idea of a conversation where the question/answer game is mediated by the musical performance that we have called "Sound Dialogues" (Scribano et al., 2014). All of them aimed at creating, developing, and experimenting with devices for capturing sensibilities.

Since 2005, after expressive resources were explored in protests and collective actions, several questions were opened that breathed a powerful air that drove the journey that is narrated here. While this was taking shape, *some paths towards qualitative research from the expressive* began to be explored. Under the conviction that when entering the *world* of expressiveness concerning the qualitative inquiry of the social world, a series of questions or theoretical and methodological work areas immediately open up. In the beginning, three problems were solved: the one that indicates that the aforementioned strategies are not data collection techniques, the one connected with the actions of the researcher who decides to work these ways to capture the social, and the fundamental question of how to register "feelings". What was written used the figure of the researcher as an agent of the action of research under the assumption that this denomination involves and assumes that it is a *collective-doing-to-do* to build knowledge about social reality. Later the journey revolved around the possibilities of elaborating *knowledge through bodies*. Pointing out/recognizing that in recent years, one of the most relevant aspects in the field of inquiry strategies in the social sciences in Latin America, is the express focus on the *use* and *rescue* of the body and its senses as the basis for such strategies. Emphasizing that in tension, always difficult, between epistemic assumptions, methodological recommendations, and redesign of observation processes, the practices of "capturing" meaning have been moving towards the capacities of the bodies themselves and their sensible potentialities. It was noted that while theatre, dance, performance, and music increasingly occupied the social scenes of production and reproduction of social structure, they have gradually become processes and mediations for observation. In this context, it was argued that the use of sensible and bodily mediations for social inquiry is based (at least partially) on three central features of the social sciences today: a) the "extension" of the epistemic definitions of the connection between perception, observation, and scientific knowledge, b) the reconceptualization of the relationships between the expression of the meaning of the action and the processes of expressiveness of sensibilities, and c) the scientific appropriation of technological and artistic means to observe the social. The multiple moorings, the furrows travelled, and the experiences had would make it very extensive to account for each port, each point of departure and arrival; of all those who accompanied, and of all those who remained at some point in the itinerary.

In this search flow, we proposed the DCE, which was designed as space for subjects to express and interpret their emotions in the context of social research. DCE are a set of inquiry practices that are articulated with a set of creativity practices connected by the active participation of the subjects involved in them. DCE tie the use of video, colours, collage, and drawing.

In this framework, we developed the *Danced Interview* which refers to the connections between expressiveness, through dance/movement, and what the subjects *know* about the social – whose modality can be summed up in the simplicity of being an interview whose questions are answered with movement.

In the same direction, we used the *Sound Dialogues* whose central motivation was to *play* as an interlude and interstice in what is in hiatus/bridge music between the word and expressiveness as a cognitive/affective way to explore the social world. The experience was carried out under the coverage of what we know in sociology about music as a device to know the social, the use of video in conducting interviews, and the set of standardized processes to investigate various social problems from art.

In addition, we also explored the "Eating Experiences" (Scribano et al., 2014) whose objective is to investigate some of the practices of feeling that are associated with food. In this context, we explore a) the relationship between food, colour, and sensations, b) the connections between colour and previous eating experiences, c) the place of the visual in flavours, and d) what are the existing links between food and society.

The situation of creating implies the biography of the subjects that are involved, the material existence conditions, and the social valuations of the act of creating. If you think of biography, it is a form of writing. That's why when I tell you my story, I enable you to enter my autonomy. What is the last limit that we usually give up in the pericorporeal space? The opening of the meaning of the body, not so much contact. Perhaps the contact is not about history but about what it means to us. Our life is made of moments, and we trace that life in our bodies. Times when I got a scar, when I had surgery, and so on. Think of a given situation and look back and forth in your life; you will see that the points in your life that you would select are moments where you had to express something. To express can also be to remain silent; we are not talking about talking.

The situation of creating has to do with enclassification, with the sociogenesis of resources, and also with biography, with what is blocked/made possible in that biography. In these plots of feeling, the moments that you would have to tell someone else are articulated – if you wanted to allow closeness – when you have needed to be silent, speak, shout, cry, paint, or dance. In other words, to tell the story of each person, you have to tell those moments.

The material conditions of existence are the material conditions of the constitution of sensations. It is like when in our life someone tells us to "be free". This is a binding paradox: the material conditions of life tie us to imperatives from which we cannot get out, or even believe that we are getting out. This paradox is presented as an imperative that has to do with the logic of the possibilities of the situation of creating.

In other words, the resources come to life in the history of the subjects: in their biography and their material conditions of existence. Conditions of what we have elsewhere called platform sensibilities shape stock scenarios today.

Another very interesting aspect is the assessment of the act of creating. Creating is an affirmative act of autonomy that happens at the moment in which a human being decides to expose in public the sensibilities regarding certain processes, objects, or people. The massification of social networks, the digitization of creative procedures, and the new skills for appropriating skills create a creative horizon of incomparable magnitude.

The life of the subjects refers to the experience about the experience of the tension between sociability-experientiality-sensibility. To create means to be in sociabilities, experientialities, and particular sensibilities. Accepted sensibilities are not the product of a mere metaphorical transposition; they are the product of certain materiality of resources, a certain biography of the subjects, and certain material conditions of existence combined in a process that calls *creativity* the facts of autonomy.

The act of creating has another peculiarity: it moves in the world of the non-transferable in speech. When the human being creates, he is having an experience over other experiences. Creating always has a problem, referring to the tension that exists between expressing oneself, expressing what another says, and expressing what a group says. It seems that creativity is a product that arises based on certain compartments or social divisions of creative work: "I have to know music to do this; besides knowing music, I have to make good music; In addition to making good music, I have to do something that the other can listen to". One of the issues that most challenges the topic of creating is that it seems to be non-transferable, just as it is untranslatable into words. But we have to understand that creativity is transferable, in the sense that it is a production that can be produced again because it is an experience about experiences. Methodologically, we try to investigate how these transmissions are possible. The digital horizon allows skills and abilities to be connected with the qualities of the virtual as storage for them and facilitator of their use.

Can we transfer the experiences of creativity? We cannot affirm that the *what* of creativity is transferred, but we can transfer, methodologically speaking, since we can recreate an experience so that the subject has an experience. That is what a methodology based on expressiveness is all about. Methodologically, we create the conditions for that creativity to occur. The subject has the imagination that has been built collectively and socially; we, as methodologists, create the conditions for an experience of experiences.

To this, a question is added: can we translate the face-to-face methodologies to the virtual environment? The answer is yes, as long as devices such as DCEs are designed where resources and experiences are shared.

It would seem that the resources, the biographies, and the material conditions of production were predetermined. However, this act of autonomy that is creativity is linked to how the subject is inscribed in that tradition, to a biographical and social context of expressiveness.

When you think about life experiences that are naturalized for oneself, but that in other times meant true acts of recreation and creation, you realize that when we put/propose to the subjects a space where they can express themselves, this space will be tied to the own history of the experience that this have to reproduce.

Precisely because creativity is an act of autonomy, we have to see how this autonomy is inscribed in a tradition, in the contexts of appreciation, revaluation, among others, of the resources, the situation of creation, and the life of the subjects. That's why sociability and sensibilities are closely linked to this.

Just as creating is not creating *ex-nihilo* but rather it is an expression of autonomy; just as we have said that methodologically it has to do with our intention to allow subjects a space of experience about their own collective and individual experiences, we also have to associate the framework of three vectors with this logic of creativity: desire, pleasure, and enjoyment. The vector of energy displacement in time (desire), the vector of the emanation of this force of autonomy in a particular time-space (pleasure), and the logic of government and control over it (enjoyment).

Digital creativity/expressiveness takes up and enriches creativity processes and allows, for example, to explore through the device presented in this chapter, a participatory appropriation of narrating emotions.

## 6.2 The Use of Zoom: Some Suggestions to Ensure Its Selection as an Instrument of Inquiry

While we had used Zoom at least since 2016 systematically to conduct international seminars and courses, it was not until 2020 that we decided to use it as a platform to conduct social research. Our intention was (and we achieved the objective) to provide a virtual alternative to our proposal of Expressive Creative Encounters in the context of our inquiries made by WhatsApp (Scribano, 2017a), Instagram (Scribano, 2017b), or our perspective of digital ethnography (Scribano, 2020).

The benefits and limitations of Zoom in various areas of university education have already been studied, such as the work of Guzacheva (2020) on the effectiveness of its use for the teaching of technical English to medical doctors. In a similar vein, Hye Jeong Kim (2020) investigated the effects of Zoom use on English learners' reading performance.

In addition, you can also perceive critical perspectives that complicate Zoom as a device of perception as shown by the work of Costello et al. (2020). The attitudes and perceptions of students have also been evaluated before the intensive use of Zoom in educational institutions at a global level as shown in the work of Derar Serhan (2020).

Nguyen Ngoc Long and Bui Huy Khoi (2020), from the Industrial University of Ho Chi Minh City in Vietnam, recently developed a study showing the effectiveness of Zoom as a platform for education and skills training. The main objective of this study was to use the traditional TRA model combined with risk perception variables to evaluate the intention of using Zoom of students during the SARS-CoV-2 pandemic.

It should be remembered that the TRA model was proposed in 1975 by Fishbein and Ajzen and that it concentrates on the construction of a system of observation of two groups of variables, which are: a) attitudes defined as a positive or negative feeling about the achievement of an objective, and (b) subjective norms, which are the very representations of individuals' perception of the ability to achieve those goals with the product.

Colleagues from Vietnam examining the *weight* of risk variables in the TRA model find that use, attitudes, and intentions in use vary according to social instability and social conditions of application which reveals the "effectiveness" of the platform as an instrument of inquiry. It is possible to argue that according to the results of this research the use of Zoom is *context-dependent* so it is an *indicator by approximation* that will serve to study society.

Taking Zoom as an instrument for social research and especially as a tool for conducting interviews, Oliffe and his colleagues suggest the following:

> In conclusion, we predict that qualitative Zoom interviews will be a long-term affair in qualitative research, one that continues well beyond the influences of COVID-19. Moreover, the feasibility and specificities of that union will undoubtedly demand compromise (and strategic negotiations) paying close attention to the many benefits, concessions and emergent challenges residing outside what we have chronicled in the current article. Pre-empting that continued dialogue and exchange we suggest that ethical and social catches including confidentiality, informed consent and data access, security and storage are unique and omnipresent issues for Zoom interviews.
>
> *(Oliffe et al., 2021, p. 7)*

Zoom has also been the subject of inquiry into both the positive and negative factors of its use as a research tool keeping in mind the perspective of the participants.

Archibald et al. (2019) in their paper report present the results of their study on the perceptions and experiences of researchers and participants about using Zoom to conduct interviews with a geographically dispersed group in Australia. By assessing the potential usefulness of Zoom for the development of qualitative data, this study contributes to increasing awareness of methodological options available to qualitative researchers and provides practical recommendations for future applications.

Also in connection with the use of Zoom as an instrument of inquiry, Falter et al. (2022) state that:

> in conclusion, doing focus groups online using Zoom was a positive experience overall and comparable to in-person focus groups for collecting qualitative data, despite the introduction of technology. More research on participant recruitment, new technology, Zoom's security features, and Zoom's use outside of a pandemic should be further explored.
>
> *(2022, p. 1)*

In the work cited, Falter and his colleagues show a detailed list of publications that point out the *pros and cons* of online interviews that many would surely see as applicable to the use of Zoom in general. But, as in this chapter the strategy of the device that is presented moves away from digital interviews and the place of Zoom is diverse, we believe that it is not possible to apply for the same objections and benefits. The COVID-19 pandemic strongly impacted the use of Zoom in social research is attested to by the work of Marnie Howlett (2021) with the suggestive title "Looking at the 'Field' Through a Zoom Lens: Methodological Reflections on Conducting Online Research During a Global Pandemic".

Zoom has had a great impact on market research where its qualities have been investigated as a support for group interviews as in the case of LDA Research Medical Market:

> How Easy is Zoom to Use? Participants. Zoom compares favourably with other video-conferencing options. It does rely on you having a good connection though and it's frustrating if you keep dropping out. Clients. Seems to work very well. Even where there are connection problems they tend to get solved quickly, and it doesn't affect the session adversely. Researchers. Really user-friendly; just about everyone feels confident using Zoom which makes our job easier. Where there are glitches due to poor connection, everyone tends to be patient and understanding.
>
> *(LDA Research, 2021)*

In this context, it is evident how advances in communication technologies offer new opportunities for qualitative research. Among these, Zoom for a series of unique features, enhance its potential appeal to qualitative and mixed-methods researchers.

Although studies have explored the use of information and communication technologies to conduct research, few have explored the perspectives of both researchers and participants on the use of the web and videoconferencing.

Although several participants experienced technical difficulties, most described their experience in the interview as very satisfying. Zoom is generally rated as satisfactory above alternative interview media, such as face-to-face, telephone, and other video conferencing services, platforms, and products. The findings suggest the viability of Zoom as a tool for collecting qualitative data information due to its relative ease of use, data management features, and security options.

From an instrumental perspective, Zoom has a series of features that facilitate interaction: a) the blackboard where writing can be shared between the researcher, the participants, and each other; b) screen sharing allows hosts and participants to share a full desktop, phone screen, or any mobile device or a part of its screen; c) poll – this makes it possible to create single and multiple choice polls, and questions for your meeting, and hosts can download a response report after the meeting; d) reactions: enable participants to ask to speak and send basic emojis like thumbs up or clapping; e) chat: this allows you to send private or collective messages between users and hosts during the meeting.

In the horizon that the DCE is postulated as a cross between online research and research based on creativity/expressiveness, the use of Zoom involves having a suitable tool for the manifestation of emotions by the participants.

In this vein, it is possible to understand how the DCE is an effective way of meeting people who, using a virtual platform, can express their emotions and creatively narrate the basic components of a politics of sensibilities.

## 6.3 Digital Creative Experience: On the COVID-19 Pandemic Context

The DCE was carried out in six countries; in each DCE, 12 people met: six from Argentina and six from other countries (Peru, Colombia, Guatemala, Mexico, and Spain). In addition, two experiences were carried out in Argentina. We did this experience with these students for what ended up being an hour and a half to two hours. The proposal was for an hour and it was extended. We are talking about around 70 people who participated from the beginning to the end of all the DCEs.

A DCE involves three moments where an attempt is made to investigate: a) what the participants feel, b) what they perceive the people in general feel about, and c) a third moment where they are asked to express what they experienced in the DCE they just completed.

Each moment is presented in the form of a question and explained as many times as necessary, systematically safeguarding and emphasizing the role of listening to the researcher, facilitating a climate of cordiality, and respecting the committed times.

Before the DCE begins, three things are done: a) we explained the activities to be developed, b) we requested informed consent and asked for permission to record, and c) each participant is presented and makes known their gender, age, and their current occupation.

The attitude of the people in the research team must be respectful, non-intrusive, and with a great willingness to collaborate, creating a climate of relaxed exchange and avoiding any possible feeling of evaluation or search for correct answers.

The coordinator must participate as little as possible, give the floor, and ask as little as possible using the contents of the images presented as axes of consultation and guidance for the participant.

Given the type of questioning and interaction, there is no guide provided by previous questions; the task of the coordinator can be guided alternately and/or articulately by the features of objects included in the image, the horizons of understanding that are proposed, the inclusion or not of the participant, and the reference to institutional environments (school, churches, states, etc.). In the interviews, the intensity and quantity of the questions are associated with theoretical and/or empirical saturation criteria.

In the first part, they are asked to take a photo that expresses what they felt and feel in the situation of being isolated. We ask them to take a photo, then share it, and explain to us why they took it and what emotions it evokes.

The photo is an effective support for emotions, but above all *take a photo* is a 4.0 skill that is currently shared by most people who have a mobile device. In the 21st century, a significant proportion of people have become digital photographers. There are in these young people (given their class, instruction level, and inheritance) *skills* to compose a photo that evokes emotions. It is possible to notice from the photos and interpretations that young people *knew* how to express their emotions through *objects*. It becomes clear that the pandemic *intensified* emotions, with the increase in the use, realization, and experience of photographs *to make* know/feel the emotional situation of the one who expresses himself.

In the photographs, the elements that appeared the most were: the objects that surround the person, the objects of greatest use and/or emotional value, the participant's face or body, and the animals and plants that shared the environment with the participants.

In the second moment, the choice of an emoji is motivated or it can be a photo, or these elements that circulate on the networks such as stickers, etc. because the pandemic was a pandemic of networks, something that is already well worked out. This task was specifically not about how they felt but what they felt that society felt. The emoji or the sticker had to be something they said something about society.

Emojis/stickers/photos have a potential, given their re-sending, circulation, and massification, of becoming very suitable instruments to understand the accepted and acceptable sensibilities regarding the subject under investigation.

Since the "massification" of social networks, sending stickers, emojis, and photos have become a creative/expressive vehicle.

The young people who participated in the experience by identifying, selecting, and interpreting emojis created a way to describe the emotions they experienced as experienced by others. Mostly the selected emojis appeal to irony, satire, and jokes as vehicles to express shared emotions. The pandemic *emphasized* the role of social networks as channels of emotional expressiveness (and relaxation?).

The legitimacy of the emoji/stickers usually lies in having been produced by another, so it dissociates its content with the intentions of the people who propose it.

In the third instance, which was a very interesting moment, we asked them to draw a picture of their own experience: how they had felt doing this creative act. These were the three moments that were repeated with each group in the same way.

Drawing is a very personal creative practice that promotes the reflexivity of the action and that allows, through the subject's word, to begin an emotional hermeneutics in connection with what happened in the DCE.

The *pandemic situation* operated as a context of creativity; in some way, the expressiveness was facilitated, and (almost) all the participants *could* draw.

The young people who lived this experience through the drawings accepted that they experienced emotions during it and that they expressed them. Most of the drawings (and their interpretations) expressed the relationship between the emotions lived and the absence of spaces to *really show* what they felt.

This *pandemic-experience* makes visible some of the axes to understanding *digital emotions*, and the drawings show that clearly. The strokes, colours, objects, and images denoted the appropriation of a diminished subjectivity on the part of the disposition of the author.

The digital expression is connected with practices of feeling lived in and through the encounter with others via Zoom; a practice that, beyond its complex configuration, indicates that the participants experienced emotions. The DCEs make it possible at least partially to capture the emotion by making it through the drawings.

Each group was introduced and contacted in the same way, there is always a person who facilitates the first contact and sometimes it occurs with a snowball logic; a climate of listening and empathy with the person speaking is promoted and the researchers participate as little as possible in the dynamics of the experience.

A central aspect of the DCE is the dialectic between the hermeneutics of the person who expresses himself, the connection that this has with the interpretations of the other participants, and the relationship established with the experiences of others. In the DCE, the role of the researcher is minimized, and consequently, given the structure of the device, it minimizes the participation of the researcher in the interpretation. The problem of the relevance of the imputation of meaning is reduced to a minimum, turning the device into a participatory mechanism to capture sensibilities or understand emotions.

## 6.4 Drawings: Expressing Emotions

The third moment of the DCE is to ask the participants to make a drawing that evokes the emotions they encountered during the experience and then explain why that drawing connected with the emotion they wanted to manifest.

The first surprise was that very few people did not want or could not make the drawing that was proposed by the coordinator of the activity as something free of evaluation. The second feature of this moment was the plurality of textures, colours, figures, and images that were put into play, which strongly sustains the creative/expressive character of the activity. And the third surprise was that all drawings represented feeling good, when at no time the criterion of good or bad, disgust or taste, etc. was put into play when explaining what the participants were expected to do.

For this section and with the function of making the reader see at least very partially the concrete results of the DCE, we have selected some drawings to try and represent the different countries, ages, and gender of the participants.

### 6.4.1 A Before and After

*Facundo:* Well, relaxed, because if I released some feelings that I had, then I felt good, normal. If I cannot release something because it feels stuck, I feel sometimes that I can't get out.

*Adrian Scribano (AS):* What does stuck mean?

*Facundo:* That because I can't find a way to express myself or feel, or I can't find the right moment or the situation sometimes doesn't deserve it as well. This as if it were a reflection, this is if it helps me a little too.

*(DCE – Mexico, 2020, p. 29)*

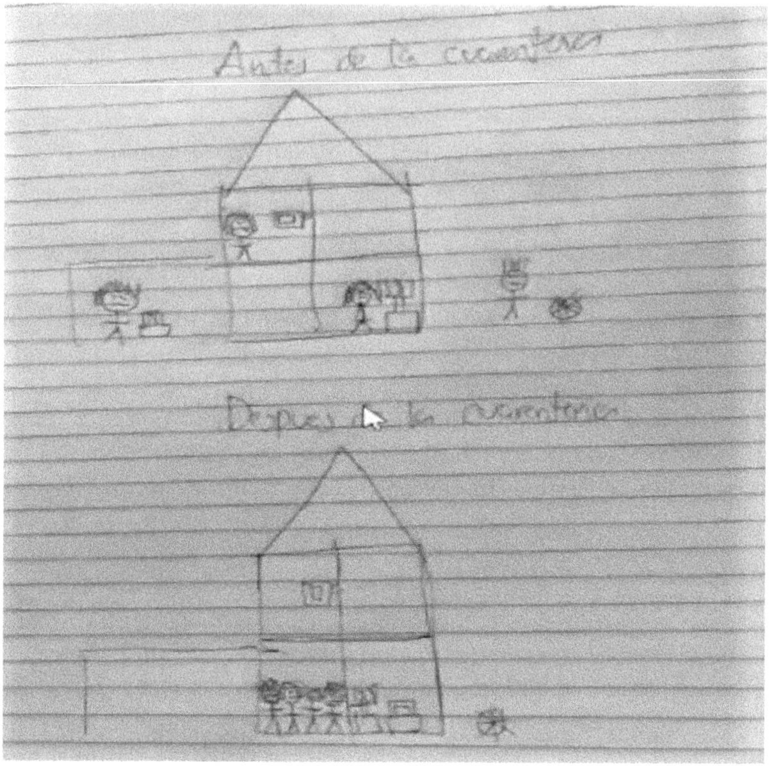

**FIGURE 6.1** Facundo (México).

Facundo makes evident how DCE helps to express emotions, as it helps to generate proximity and to be able to show what it feels like, the participants can *unlock* the regulated impossibility of not saying what happens to them.

For Facundo, as for almost all the DCE's participants, this device meant a before and after in being able to express emotions, understanding that the same things happen to many and that photos, memes, and drawings allow them "to say emotions".

Facundo's contribution demonstrates how a set of basic and simple rules build a device that allows creating different ways of narrating emotions in the context of simplicity as a criterion of validity of an effective methodology.

### *6.4.2 An Open Heart*

> Liliana: Well the drawing is like this, although the wings for the outside, for the exit are broken, there is one that has like a Band-Aid that has to do with virtuality, with this it is a good way of approach that is not the one that I would like the most, but it is a way to approach. But mainly although the subjects are anonymous, or black, we opened up in relation

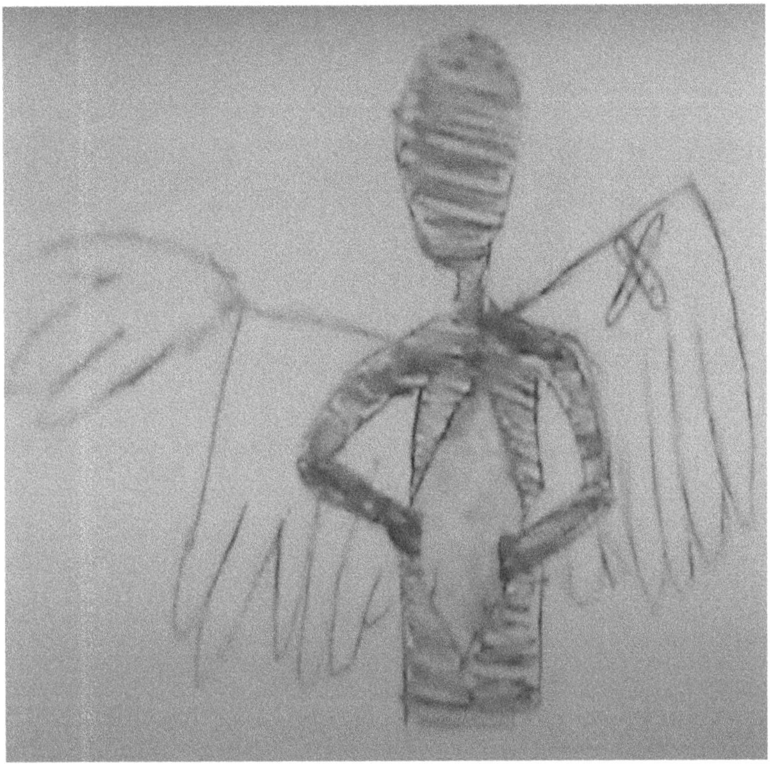

**FIGURE 6.2** Liliana (Argentina).

> to emotions. Although we are all anonymous, we all talk about something how difficult it is to talk about emotions, but in an academic field that teaches us to be rational. We had to look inside ourselves and each other; do not know each other but we could do it. And this experience of being able to deal with emotions in an academic space, I felt very good about this.
>
> *(DCE – Colombia, 2020, p. 30)*

Liliana clearly expresses the feeling of isolation that manages to break the DCE beyond living it as something partial, opening the heart and putting wings implies taking up in the modified body what is transformative in the emotions, and clearly showing the feature of them as questioning practices that demand involvement.

The DCE is transformed into spaces that make it possible to feel better and use the expressive resources that beyond the word convey repressed and forbidden emotional ecologies. Heart, wings, and an *incomplete* body speak clearly about how DCEs are devices that engage bodies/emotions as a whole.

**FIGURE 6.3** Juan Martin (Chile).

The DCE facilitate the expression of emotions, they are devices that, by demanding the simplicity of creating through emotions, become critical of a reason lost in the labyrinths of solipsism.

*Juan Martin:* This is my drawing, and well, there's one like a thinking face, like that emoji. And I drew that because I felt that the activity was still like cathartic in that sense, it was a very nice space, in which we could laugh, I personally laughed a lot. I liked their memes and the images they showed, and it was cathartic in the sense that I experienced a lot of sensations that it's still like hard to experience in social isolation. So in that sense it was a very pleasant experience and also very reflective at the same time, because as we were laughing, we were problematizing the way we have felt during this time.

*AS:* Sure.

*Juan Martin:* So I thought it was a very good experience, very beautiful, that is undoubtedly appreciated in this context of social isolation, of a way of meeting it seems to me.

*(DCE – Chile, 2020, p. 39)*

Juan Martin's narration begins by giving a clear clue to how the digital creative process works today, where a hand drawing borrows an expressive resource from the digital world specifically created to express emotions.

For Juan Martin, the DCE was a cathartic experience in the sense commonly attributed to the term allowed to express, *take out*, *loosen*: all particularities of a situation where emotions flow and become connectors with other people. A very important axis is the allusion to laughter, to *have fun*. The DCE is a social research device where people, when creating/expressing, experience a set of emotional ecologies favourable to *well-being*.

### 6.4.3 The Sun of the Encounter

*Claudia:* Let's look at this simply. Well, I felt as if I were in a warm conversation so I related it to the sun, to an attempt at sun. And a very pleasant talk, like a feeling of warmth to be able to share experiences that we are all going through, helps I think with a good attitude.

*AS:* Sure, that's good. And what did that good attitude mean?

*Claudia:* Because I think that even though we all feel a sense of anxiety [about isolation] or the desire to go out, we are continuing to work on our studies, at school, we avoid contact with our families [because of the pandemic], then for me that is having a good attitude.

*(DCE – México, 2020, p. 26)*

The DCE are spaces of interaction that generate warmth and good weather in the context of the anguish and stress of the participants; as Claudia says it is an experience of a pleasant talk. The hermeneutics of Claudia associating warmth with the sun clearly shows how the people who participate in the DCE appeal to their disposition as authors in their own geometry.

### 6.4.4 Sharing Intensity

*Paula:* This is my little drawing, it was like in the end each one on his screen, but there was a stronger connection than the screen, this is the summary.

*AS:* You don't have to summarize it; how do you feel the connection? How would you explain it?

*Paula:* That in the end we are all like almost the same, we have similar feelings within the confinement and all that, in some way

*AS:* And how did you feel in the experience?

*Paula:* Well, I mean, I felt a little more understood perhaps, like being able to talk about it but also being able to laugh.

*(DCE – Chile, 2020, p. 28)*

Computers transmit intensity is Paula's message, which takes up with this phrase the connection between impression, perception, and sensation that implies all

**FIGURE 6.4** Claudia (Mexico).

emotion and transfers it to a virtual /mobile/digital relationship. Her drawing is interpreted by her as a mechanism of connection that allows sharing similar emotions in the horizon of geocultural and geopolitical differences.

DCEs are devices that make it possible to capture what is moving in emotions in terms of conditions that transform the world (*sensu* Sartre). Movement and transformations of the real are now observed in the virtual/mobile/digital world.

### *6.4.5 Emotions like Birds*

*Emilio:* Yes, it's me. How I seek to show feeling in this drawing is that on the one hand having expressed what I felt, something that I have not done in all these weeks is to express that feeling that the window in my drawing shows

*AS:* Yes

*Emilio:* They've come out, I don't know if it was noticed, but my voice was choppy. It was difficult for me, it was difficult for me to speak what I

**FIGURE 6.5** Paula (Chile).

> thought, but I could. And in that way, with these small pieces of birds or pieces of paper, I try to symbolize that I have let those emotions out of my body, my mind also, and at the same time during this talk, new sensations, emotions, thoughts have entered thanks to the contributions of other participants and it is like a cycle of harmony of entry and exit of sensations that I have had in those moments. (DCE – Perú, 2020, p. 24)

DCEs are moments that enable expressiveness by putting the beginning of expression in a nonverbal register. Here it is shown how there is a flow between listening to the interpellation of the coordinator, identifying the need to express oneself, drawing, and then interpreting. The experience of saying what he feels is perceived in a cycle of harmony with the other participants and what Emilio calls their testimonies. It's clear: DCEs are moments where you feel saying what you feel.

The participants of the DCE experience how the emotions *come out* of their bodies and like Emilio associate them with birds and papers that carry inscribed what they feel; to reinforce the character of the message that emotions have.

FIGURE 6.6 Emilio (Peru).

## 6.5 Some Schematic Final Remarks

Digital Creative Experiences allow us to capture very effectively the emotions of the participants. The sensibilities that they perceived were present in the other people during the confinements imposed by the COVID-19 pandemic.

One of the recurring features in all the DCEs was that people expressed their confidence and tranquillity, empathy with others, and amazement at the procedure, as they appreciated that with in such a simple way, they could communicate their emotions.

1. Uncertainty as an expression of ignorance about COVID-19, as a result of not being able to complete what was planned, and the uncertainty of the duration of sanitary measures.
2. The daily experience of the *roller coaster feeling* of going from euphoria to stillness, to depression and then back to euphoria ... reproduced at least once a day.
3. The experience of various intensities of sadness, a feeling of confinement, frustration, and anger, creating a discouraging painting of the world.

4. The experience of being faced with an opportunity: of doing something that they had never been able to do, of expressing themselves in ways that they had not thought of before, stopping doing things, helping, being valued for something, etc.
5. Finally, the feeling of reconstruction of family ties and definition of closeness with friends, loves, ideologies, etc.

It is in this panorama of the politics of sensibilities that we can better understand what we have already stated: the common characteristics in terms of politics of sensibilities are fear, anxiety, uncertainty, anguish, and sadness.

## References

Archibald, M. M., Ambagtsheer, R. C., Casey, M. G., & Lawless, M. T. (2019). Using zoom videoconferencing for qualitative data collection: Perceptions and experiences of researchers and participants. *International Journal of Qualitative Methods, 18*, 1–8. https://doi.org/10.1177/1609406919874596

Costello, E., Brown, M., Donlon, E., & Girme, P. (2020). 'The pandemic will not be on zoom': A retrospective from the year 2050. *Postdigital Science and Education, 2*, 619–627. https://doi.org/10.1007/s42438-020-00150-3

Falter, M. M., Arenas, A. A., Maples, G. W., Smith, C. T., Lamb, L. J., Anderson, M. G., Uzzell, E. M., Jacobs, L. E., Cason, X. L., Griffis, T. A. N., Polzin, M. & Wafa, N. Z. (2022). Making room for Zoom in focus group methods: Opportunities and challenges for novice researchers (during and beyond COVID-19). *Forum: Qualitative Social Research, 23*(1), 1–27. http://dx.doi.org/10.17169/fqs-23.1.3768

Fishbein, M., & Ajzen, I. (1975). *Belief, Attitude, Intention, and Behavior: An Introduction to Theory and Research*. Addison-Wesley.

Guzacheva, N. (2020). Zoom technology as an effective tool for distance learning in teaching English to medical students. *Bulletin of Science and Practice, 6*(5), 457–460. https://doi.org/10.33619/2414-2948/53/61

Howlett, M. (2021). Looking at the 'field' through a zoom lens: Methodological reflections on conducting online research during a global pandemic. *Qualitative Research, 22*(3), 387–402. https://doi.org/10.1177/1468794120985691

Kim, H. (2020). The efficacy of zoom technology as an educational tool for english reading comprehension achievement in EFL classroom. *International Journal of Advanced Culture Technology, 8*(3), 198–205. https://doi.org/10.17703/IJACT.2020.8.3.198

LDA Research. (2021). *The Pros and Cons of Using Zoom for Qualitative Research*. Retrieved from: https://www.ldaresearch.com/what-we-do/

Long, N. N., & Khoi, B. H. (2020). The intention to study using zoom during the SARS-CoV-2 pandemic. *International Journal of Emerging Technologies in Learning (iJET), 15*(21), 195–216. https://doi.org/10.3991/ijet.v15i21.16777

Oliffe, J. L., Kelly, M. T., Gonzalez Montaner, G., & Yu Ko, W. F. (2021). Zoom interviews: Benefits and concessions. *International Journal of Qualitative Methods*, 1–8. https://doi.org/10.1177/16094069211053522

Scribano, A. (2011). Vigotsky, Bhaskar and Thom: Traces for the understanding (and foundation) of the Experiencing Units. *RELMIS-Latin American Journal of Social Research Methodology, 1*(1), 21–35.

Scribano, A. (2013). Expressive creative encounters: A strategy for sociological research of expressiveness. *Global Journal of Human Social Sciences, 13*(5), 33–38.

Scribano, A. (2014). Danced interview: Narration of an unfinished journey. *Interstices, 8*(2), 103–112.

Scribano, A. (2017a). Miradas cotidianas. El uso de Whatsapp como experiencia de investigación social. *Revista Latinoamericana de Metodología de la Investigación Social, 13*(7), 8–22.

Scribano, A. (2017b). Instaimagen: mirar tocando para sentir. *Revista Brasileira de Sociologia da Emoção (RBSE), 16*(47), 45–55.

Scribano, A. (2020). El amor filial como práctica intersticial: Una etnografía digital. *Empiria. Revista de Metodología de las Ciencias Sociales, 47,* 129–151.

Scribano, A., Boragnio, A., Bertone, J., & Lava, P. (2014). Traces of a methodological innovation: 'Experiences of eating', a process in production. *NORUS: Novos Rumos Sociológicos, 2,* 80–103.

Serhan, D. (2020). Transitioning from face-to-face to remote learning: Students' attitudes and perceptions of using Zoom during COVID-19 pandemic. *International Journal of Technology in Education and Science (IJTES), 4*(4), 335–342.

# 7

# TOWARDS AN EPISTEMOLOGY OF THE DIGITAL RESEARCH OF EMOTIONS

## Introduction

As it has been noted from the introduction to the previous chapter, it is at least unnecessary to establish the difference between the real and the virtual; the world of virtual/mobile/digital life provides at the same time the adequate tools to know the world in general and to know oneself, and, in this context, it is possible to sustain the existence of digital emotions.

There are several approaches to analyzing the relationships between emotions and epistemology: some affirm the affective component of emotional experience plays an essential explanatory role in the acquisition of evaluative knowledge (Vanello, 2020), or some work against "epistemic perceptualism", about the view that emotional experiences, as involving a perception of value, can constitute reasons for evaluative belief (Mitchell, 2017), or some argue that there is a plausible non-epistemic understanding of the view that emotions are evaluative modes (Müller, 2017).

There are various epistemological and philosophical reflections on intellectual practices in digital scenarios, such as the case of Marteleto (2015) on writing on websites or that of Thomson-Jones and Moser (2019) on digital art.

It is also possible to identify works that over-articulate epistemic analysis from the Global South with the digital, such as that of De Vasconcelos Gico and Hecker Luz (2017), and others that are oriented to the structure of digital technology (García Gutiérrez, 2011).

In a different sense but concurrent to what this chapter intends to suggest, it is possible to find works on platforms, networks, or the virtual/mobile/digital world and emotions, for example the research of Baquero Rodríguez and his colleagues entitled "The Construction of Facebook as an Affective Prosthesis"

DOI: 10.4324/9781003319771-8

(2014). Also, works by Basabe de Quintale and Durán Rodríguez (2013) connect Facebook and emotions.

Social networks have been explored as fundamental factors of knowledge management around the commodification of life, as in the case of Grützmann and colleagues, who conclude: "The virtual social networks are a growing phenomenon and the content produced by consumers with innovative behavior is especially important for management of knowledge directed toward innovation" (Grützmann et al., 2013, p. 218).

In this context, this book reviews various practices of knowledge that involve theoretical, epistemic, and methodological consequences that, in some sense, are systematized in this section.

For us, emotions as practices that transform the world have a direct impact on how we feel about the world, and this gives them a strongly epistemic trait because in and through them we know the world.

The cognitive-affective structure of our emotions involves, as we developed in Chapter 1, some politics of the senses, some politics of sensibilities, and some particular units of experience associated with a space/time that also involve particular geo-cultures and geopolitics.

In this final chapter, we want to return to the connections that exist in the emotional ecologies that have emerged in the previous chapters, emotions as texts, and the virtual/mobile/digital world that brings us closer to a hermeneutics of the practices of feeling.

In this direction a) we reconstruct the "partial conclusions" of the tools and devices exposed in the framework of digital research on emotions, b) we present trust and consumption as key feeling practices to understand Society 4.0, and finally c) we expose hope as an example of the implication of a critique of Society 4.0 within the framework of the epistemic features of emotions and their importance in the virtual/mobile/digital world.

## 7.1 Epistemic Reconstruction

Here is presented an outline of the connections between virtual/mobile/digital world and emotions followed by the reconstruction of the epistemic consequences of what is stated in the book.

### *7.1.1 Digital Emotions, Society 4.0, and Social Research*

Social research has been characterized since the 19th century by the modification of instruments of inquiry based on the "rhythm" of the modifications of the social structuration process; the first 20 years of the 21st century repeat this connection and impact on the epistemic view of the social sciences in a general way.

The view on Society 4.0 as a Moebius strip takes us to the present and the recent "crossing" between the social structuration process and the so-called Revolution 4.0. In the last 15 years, the entire planet has been modified for various and multiple reasons. Here we will only refer to three of the greatest changes in connection with emotions: 1) economic modifications, 2) changes in the coordination of action processes, and 3) the consolidation of a special politics of the sensibilities. In the context of what we suggest in Chapter 1, the following have a single goal: to emphasize the place and role of emotions and sensibilities to build an epistemological reflexive scenery.

1. Society 4.0 is associated with Industry 4.0, which is understood as a stage of digitization of the manufacturing sector, driven by four modifications: more data managed by industrial companies, powerful and cheap computers, greater analytical capacity, and developments in interactions between people and machines, from artificial intelligence to androids and robots to production through 3D printers. The reduction of costs, the improvements in the production lines, and the use of new databases are some of the central results derived from such modifications. In this framework, the economy is transformed and supported more and more in perceptual modifications, the massification of practices of digital emotions, and digital management of sensibilities.
2. Another factor that has transformed social life is the appearance and consolidation of social networks as a vehicle for interaction and coordination of action. From Facebook, WhatsApp, and Instagram to Tinder and Twitter, knowing, finding, meeting, loving, and hating other people is done digitally/virtually. Social networks and platforms enable us to produce, locate, send, pay, and consume everything from food to medicine, from drinks to sex, from religions to the management of births, marriages, and deaths. What was previously only done in squares, bars, restaurants, theatres, schools, stadiums, parks, chapels, cemeteries, etc., today can be done in and through the mobile phone, tablet, PC, or any kind of digital device. On this horizon appears a digital socialization where beliefs, social norms, rules of courtesy, and laws have changed as well as crime, threat, violence, harassment, and so many other forms of aggression, discrimination, and injustice. These new sociabilities also imply modifications in the experiences and sensibilities that we will see in the next section, but for now, let us pause to reflect on a few modifications of these sociabilities.
3. In Society 4.0, politics of sensibilities have also been modified, creating a "sensibility of platform". We have addressed elsewhere the direct relationship between digital work, planetary structuring process and politics of sensibilities, and the emergence of sensibilities of platform.

*(Scribano & Lisdero, 2019)*

> A politics of sensibilities (...) is understood as the set of cognitive-affective social practices aimed at the production, management and reproduction of horizons of action, disposition, and cognition. These horizons refer: (1) to the organization of daily life (...), (2) to the information to

> order preferences and values (...), and (3) to the parameters for time/space management.
>
> *(De Sena & Scribano, 2020, p. 40)*

In this context, Society 4.0 more than the transformations already mentioned, involves, among others aspects, two central features that constitute "sensibilities of platform": one around the experience of the house and another about connection to general (and global) consumption.

### *7.1.2 Emotions and Epistemology*

There are diverse ways to systematize the theoretical orientations on which the studies on emotion and epistemology are based (Scribano & Korstanje, 2017), and, in the same vein, there are multiple forms to build the bridge between emotions and knowledge.

Brun and Kuenzle have written that we can "distinguish five epistemic functions that have been claimed for emotions: motivational force, salience and relevance, access to facts and beliefs, non-propositional contributions to knowledge and understanding, and epistemic efficiency" (Brun & Kuenzle, 2018, p. 1).

There are at least three features that transform emotions into an epistemological topic par excellence. Firstly, emotions are a way of knowing the world, secondly, emotions are metaphors for relationships between human beings, the world, and other living beings, and thirdly they are practices that transform the world.

In the first sense, emotions allow us to know what the world is since it configures an important part of our capacity, as human beings, to explain and understand the time-space in which we live and to account for the geopolitical and cultural particularities of that world. The connection between impression, perception, and sensation is how human beings grasp and interpret the structure in which we move. Through the senses, we identify, select, and order the world. The imputations we make based on what we see, smell, like, feel, and hear are organizational schemes that allow us to accept and transform the structure in which we live. In this direction, a critique of established modes of feeling is a critique of the acceptable modes of understanding, this being the basis for understanding that there is of logos in the pathos of emotions. The organizational texture that the emotions provide to the impression-perception-sensation triangle configures a web of feelings and senses that tell us what the world is and how it can remain and/or transform.

In the second sense, emotions are a metaphor for our relationships with the world for three reasons: a) because they allows us to move what we have perceived to areas that we have not yet explored, b) because they make it possible to understand processes, objects, and people through qualities of some and of others that they evoke, make reference to, and make objects and people present to other processes, and c) because they reflect narratives about the world that we have in a sense close to speech, representation, and imagination.

There is a "back and forth" between metaphor, narration, and emotions as a central part of knowing. An example of this is what Russell Hochschild has written about it:

> One way to get to feeling is through the story to which it is attached. Deep feelings are linked to a deep story. As I use the term, a deep story is a narrative based on a core metaphor evoking a given range of emotions. As in a dream, it is based on a telling scene. We take facts out of the deep story. We take moral ideals out of the deep story. What remains is the evocative power of the deep story itself – the objective correlative of given deep feelings.
>
> *(Russell Hochschild, 2019, p. 13)*

In the third sense, given that emotions are actions that disrupt the states of affairs, they become central features of practical logics (*sensu* Bourdieu) that allow the world and life to pass through, that make it possible to identify an order, a nomos, and a system and its pathways of construction, crisis, and change. To "be in the world" is to feel the world, it is a tribute to the experience – experience and existence of human beings and their particular way of relating to what is given in and through the order/change dialectic.

### 7.1.3 Theoretical-Epistemic Consequences of the Tools Presented in the Book

This section summarizes the "epistemic conclusions" that each chapter leaves and that allows the elaboration of a puzzle about the connection between emotions, knowledge, and inquiry strategies.

#### 7.1.3.1 Cognitive/Affective Consequences of Looking by Touching

As we have suggested in the Introduction of this book, we are immersed in a process that has come to be known as Revolution 4.0, and this is strongly associated with what we call the touch era.

The social forms of immediacy entail specific surfaces where conditions of particular experiences are taken for granted and sociabilities are assumed. The immediate is a special "here-now" that redefines the present.

The conditions of productivity and the commodification of sensations are united in a common "pre-origin" that is elaborated in "using the body" to relate to the instruments/machines/apparatus.

Social practices acquire the texture of the materiality of the body/emotion, the density of sensation, and the processing of the senses. The social ways of connecting with the world have been transferred to the hands, the fingers, the fingertips, first of all with the instruments of communication, but also with the means of payment, entertainment devices, and the devices for cooking and cleaning. We literally live by pressing keys, sliding, tapping, and "clicking"; thus our day-to-day is populated by cell phones, credit cards, transportation payment cards, kitchens, microwaves, etc. which are used across social classes, genders, ethnicities, and ages. Societies that paradoxically become spectacularized and at the same time focus on the individual, that get excited "about everything" but that are limited to those closest to them, are societies that redefine the politics of touch, the conditions of the rules of touching, touch, and being touched.

All the politics of the senses are activities to solve situations (*sensu* Thomas), of being successful in the social presentation of the person (*sensu* Goffman), and elaborate the knowledge at hand (*sensu* Schütz) that the subjects use in and from the world of life. It is in the context of the aforementioned policies that touch becomes relevant.

Social relations have moved towards a metaphor of "touching", of "clicking", and of interacting with instruments. The subjects express themselves by moving, "submerging" sensible parts of the apparatus, and with this action, rather than seeing or doing, it is necessary to know "how to touch". This is an approximation to the reality that, although it does not eliminate "knowing how" and "knowing what" (typical of the 20th-century dispute), redefines access to the world.

A digital age where the line between the superfluous, prostheses, and body extensions are diluted with the "friendliness" of the interfaces to buy/enjoy. Knowing how to touch is more than a skill, it is a condition of the cognitive/affective possibility of being in the world.

The 21st century will be a century "of touching", and the social sciences will have the obligation to redefine (themselves) in terms of their strategies of inquiry and ontological discussions. In these contexts, actor, agent, subject, and author will be reconfigured, and consequently what is in them of public positionality will also be modified.

In this mode of interaction, human beings are elaborating a grammar of vision as a diverse code of the word. The "instaimage" is a proposal to live an experience from immersion in a scenario that transits the sensibilities and where sensoriality is the vehicle to build images with our hands.

It is the image makers who, determined to communicate sensorialities, redefine the experience of feeling in and with the image. They are actors in daily productions where the features of the new "visual literacy" are played, they are subjects that with the "camera at hand" are always in a position to produce the ICI effect (immersion, connectivity, and intensity).

After reviewing some of the most important aspects of the epistemic features of the impact of the image on the digital and vice versa, some methodological reflections follow regarding what is exposed in this book.

#### *7.1.3.2 Methodological Impacts of a Horizon Observation*

Intuitively, we could argue that *seeing* connects with perceiving that alludes to knowing by presence: the subject looks passively. The unknown is made clearer when we look in and through an object that is far away from us. Given that the activity of "controlling" seeing is inherent, being able to "take different positions in a scene" in a more "complete" way than only using sight allows us to be less passive.

In dialectical relationship with "seeing", there is *looking*, on which we could advance preliminarily as the action of directing the view to an object, to its inscription horizon , and to that of the observer himself, concentrating, focusing, and taking them into consideration as parts of the object of a scene. Also here, drones deconstruct the gaze due to their capacity for simultaneity (they can look at the object, the position of the object, and the observer at the same time), and instantaneity.

Finally, *observation* is also modified, since the drone expands the ability to "examine closely", radically enhancing the possibilities of recording, saving, and tracking that every observer considers.

The tensions between seeing, looking, and observing that Society 4.0 brings have a full impact on the capabilities that drones grant to social research.

Recapitulating what we have stated so far, it is possible to synthesize the following features of the use of drones: a) they are eyes that fly and that can form an imperceptible buzz "over" daily life, b) they are instruments to see things happening that "stretch" the current paradigm of sensibility, playing the role of witnesses of reality from a distance, c) they are new social actors managed remotely – they modify the ecology of social practices involving non-human agents, d) they are part of the dictum of daily life in the 21st century: "to see is to make you feel", e) they are the cause of "new" spaces for socialization in societies where novelty characterizes social networks and everyday life, f) they are operators to record social, individual, and collective practices –the technological capabilities for data storage and management stand out, g) they are the cause of dimensional, perspective, and displacement unlocking, and h) they are spurs that challenge us to rethink the boundaries between seeing, looking, and observing.

In this context, the well-known connections between proximity and distance, and the important aspects of daily life and social research are modified. Among the most obvious modifications, the following can be highlighted:

1. The "qualification"/measure of the closeness/distance between the subjects is transformed into the power to construct part of the politics of the gaze that, together with social and personal communication networks, disrupt what is experienced by looking.
2. The policies of touch, something close to the development that has already taken place with time/space unlocking, is obtained by communication via the Internet.
3. The observations of human beings and between human beings and other living beings, in terms of bearing witness to life and ways of life. Drones come to complement the radical transformations in the visualization processes initiated by digitization, the Internet, and mobile communication, producing

> substantial modifications in the experience of proximity/distance. In this sense, the beginning of the 21st century prompts us to return to an age-old question about who and how we will consider a neighbour, and about the ways we view them.

In this century, the interaction between Society 4.0, social networks, and drones leaves us with a well-known practice that can be summarized as follows: tell me how you look at me and I'll tell you how we feel. Look, truth, and technology once again challenge our capacities to exercise epistemic vigilance and indicate a critical direction for the social sciences to go in.

#### *7.1.3.3 Instantaneity and Knowledge*

The experience that we have reported and discussed brings us back to the path of questions/answers about which the social sciences continue to think. The "Everyday Gaze" implies exploring ontologies without metaphysical dogmas; reflecting on instruments without reifying them, and epistemically monitoring the fetishization of our findings.

##### 1. "Faithfully register", or realism of the registry

Since its inception, the social sciences have been traversed by a set of discussions around "faithfully registering", or regarding the realism of the registry. This early topic of disagreement included: theories of perception, approaches to subjectivity, methodological perspectives on recording, etc. With the spread of networks such as WhatsApp, the renewal of the dispute over realism and constructivism becomes a requirement for the understanding of the multiple worlds we inhabit and live in.

##### 2. Place of who registers and who publishes

The use of WhatsApp forces us to rethink roles in investigation – more precisely, in fieldwork and editing work. An interview is recorded on a tape recorder (it can also be on the telephone), and the interviewer takes notes (most of the time), but the person who records and edits is not necessarily the researcher. This situation changes with the cell phone or tablet. The observation is registered/edited in each informative "entry". In this way, what is common to qualitative research is radicalized: observation is already an interpretation. Another problem that is renewed with the use of WhatsApp is how and to what extent an observation is a translation and a hermeneutic event in itself. "Daily Glances" has been an experience full of decision-making: what to record, which surface inscription to use, which edge to select to display, and what we want to conceptually transmit/witness. I saw it, I recorded it, and I reported it is a tripod that makes the work of double hermeneutics of social research and the constant surveillance of our preconceptions and naturalizations that require theoretical and epistemic translations very evident. In this way, the theory/information/record game demands a resolution at each moment of observation.

### 3. Voice, image, text, and "virtuality"

A feature of WhatsApp is that the recording surfaces are multiple and juxtaposed. The researcher can record his description of a situation, take a photo of it, film a video, incorporate text, and copy information produced by others from the Internet. This possibility implies that, in a particular and limited way, the researcher, standing at the vertex where the vectors of said surfaces converge, can "reproduce" the real with many features of "the action being done".

### 4. Translation effects: "I'm seeing it"

Another problem that is renewed with the use of WhatsApp is how and to what extent an observation is a translation and a hermeneutical event in itself. "Everyday Glances" has been a highly charged decision-making experience: what to record, which way to record it, which side to display, and what conceptually we want to convey/testify. I saw it, recorded it, and reported it. It is a tripod that makes the double hermeneutic work of social research very evident, and with it the constant monitoring of our presumptions and conditioning that require theoretical and epistemic explanation.

As we have argued elsewhere:

> the use of sensory and bodily mediations for social inquiry is based (at least partially) on three central features of the Social Sciences today: a) the "broadening" of epistemic definitions of the connection between perception, observation and scientific knowledge; b) the reconceptualization of the relationships between the expression of the meaning of action and the processes of expressiveness of sensibilities; and c) the scientific appropriation of technological and artistic means to observe the social.
>
> *(Scribano, 2016, p. 68)*

### *7.1.3.4 Digital Creativity Paths 4.0 of Collective Research*

As we have seen in the chapter on digital creative experiences, communication applications such as Zoom go beyond the mere instrumental role of facilitating temporally and spatially untethered interaction. For each of the moments of the experience, it is possible to extract some effective cognitive consequence, on the one hand, and epistemological, on the other.

At the moment when people are asked to photograph themselves, it brings out the set of emotions that they experienced during confinement in the pandemic. At least three consequences can be specified: firstly, the subject who is questioned becomes a hermeneutic. On the one hand, the creator has to synthesize and to map the emotions experienced, and therefore, in a fairly short period, identify them, systematize them, and give them a sense where experience, sociability, and sensibility constitute the context of selection of the emotion. But, on the other hand, and in the frame of the person's geometry, accentuates the authorial moment of creatively expressing with the photo the emotions interpreted. As we have seen in other parts of this book, taking a photo is a moment of knowing that there are two senses: in a basic sense, in terms of what one can see in the photo, and in an experiential one, what it is that he wants to do with the photo. And that is why from the first moment in the Digital Creative Experiences it appears the geometry of the authoring person, how articulating the other moments the individual, the actor, the agent, and the subject, could express in this doing the photo. An event is taking place that allows us to know the world, emphasizing whether emotions are maps of the world, and the way we express our emotions are the cartographies of that world, and that in the context the digital ones occur to reference the movements of people living in the world.

In the second moment of these experiences, the participating subject is asked to identify a meme, sticker, or photo selected from the set of iconographic productions, photographs, and videos that appeared during the pandemic that evokes what they perceive society felt in those moments. In this way, the participant exercises the interpretive capacity as a reader of the "creative/expressive sources" of society. At this moment, you can perceive the development of "new cognitive skills" that must be developed to be able to understand the world. These are skills that allow experiences to be identified, and solving situations because the others produce images so that another person can continue in the situation, summarizing the bridges that the circulation of the image has created between an unimaginable number of experiences, from the weight of creative expression. This when the social media application allows the person to solve situations based on digital information from the digital creation, and in the context of digital circulation. If there is a moment of the methodological instruments that we have presented in this book where the mobile/virtual/digital cannot be differentiated from the real in binary form, it is at the moment of interpreted, digital creativity where, with an image, we all perceive and experience something similar, which is accepted almost unnoticed, and the creative act becomes a cognitive act that allows resolving the set of relationships of my experience, my life lived, and my existence in the world.

Finally, it is clear that when we ask the subjects to make a drawing, creativity and expressiveness already transcend the limits of skill and recreate images where authorship and agency meet subjectivity. The cognitive subject is the creative subject that creates the ties that connect the societal with the individual and the authorial.

#### *7.1.3.5 Knowing by Experiencing the Virtual/Mobile/Digital*

If there is a quality of digital ethnography, it is the global use of living an immersive experience in a community and/or a group, in and through digital media.

Digital Creative Experiences should provide a warning in the use of the methodological approaches that we have discussed, but especially in digital ethnography, where the notion of experience and the notion of existence is redefined. Thus, three bands of the same Moebius tape are constituted, which allows the knowing person to experience the digital world.

A central aspect of the experience in and through the digital is the way of experience as subjective appropriation of sharing the gaze of the other. In the research about love as collective action, "feeling" strongly motivated the energy that the collectives wanted to transmit in their "interventions" in the virtual/mobile/digital world. There is a redefinition of the possible connections between empathy, sympathy, and emotion as criteria for identification, selection, and analysis of emotions associated with conflict networks where love was the main energy of collective practice.

On the other hand, the action and notion of "having an experience" are impacted by at least three factors: a) based on previous digital experiences, in terms of having used applications or spaces like the analysis of hyperlinks of web pages, blogs, engines, etc., b) the proposal of "participation" on its surface to describe the organization and/or registered subject in terms of "leaving a message", answering surveys, etc., and c) the alternatives provided in the digital world such as giving likes, expressing taste, leave emoticons, etc.

A third element constitutes the transformation of experiencing, exploring, following traces, elaborating circumstances of interaction, asking/responding to the recording surface from the experiences, and experiences as we have finished analyzing them.

In these senses, virtual ethnography is a modality of sharing certainties, doubts, and knowledge with those that we propose to study in a similar but not identical way to that in a face-to-face practice of "natural" co-presence.

In any case, it is in virtual ethnography where it is best understood that there is no possible disconnection between the real and the virtual and that all social science research in this century will be in one way or another a multi-method strategy.

## 7.2 Trust and Digital Consumption: Two Practices of Feeling with Epistemological Implications

In this section, the purpose is to make evident how trust and consumption as practices of feeling have a direct impact on the ways of knowing and the possibilities of observing. Trust in the context of the emotional ecology links optimism, pessimism, and fear, while the feeling of consuming is part of the emotional ecology of enjoyment, joy, and containment (Scribano, 2017, 2021).

### *7.2.1 Digital Trust: Certainties, Knowledge, and "Plurality Management"*

Trust is a practice of feeling that acquires different forms depending on the geopolitics and geo-cultures in which it occurs. Perhaps two of the clearest examples are the place that trust has in China (Barbalet, 2014) and the different way it manifest in the West (Sztompka, 1999).

The acts of "having" or "giving" trust are one of the dialectical axes between the sociology of knowledge and a political epistemology about how human beings understand the world, and how we behave with other living beings and nature. Like all emotions, trust has a cognitive-affective structure that from sensibility is linked to knowing.

Trust is structured around three key factors: belief, taking risks, and taking for granted/being sure about something.

There are two ways of understanding the place of *belief in the generation of trust*: believing in the other and believing with the other. Believing is a cognitive-affective action in the existence of coherence between what is supposed/expected and the results of the action of another and/or others. People believe "with" others "and/or" others since, by definition, belief is a shared practice that creates sociability and common experience. Believing in others and with others elaborates a special politics of sensibility that disputes the monopoly of truth to the political economy of morality.

Another factor is that the generation of trust is carried out directly through "taking the risk" of expecting coherence and reciprocity from others. People rely on the fulfilment of a promise, the intentions of the other, and the commitment to the problem that brings them together. Human beings learn to balance risk and reliability as a daily management modality: we trust that what is expected will happen.

On the other hand, trusting someone or some expert system implies *taking for granted* that the states of affairs tend to repeat themselves; people believe because they assume that someone or something will act as long as they are expected to do so. They take for granted the reproduction of life as they know it: that is, they trust. The breakdown of this trust is the root but also the symptom of social crises.

Along the same lines, trust is presented as a possibility of stabilizing expectations: reliability in the politics of the senses, security in expert systems, and as predictability of errors.

Human beings trust someone (and/or something) when their connection is based on the predictive ability of the results of their senses. Smelling, touching, tasting, hearing, and seeing allow us to know the world, and these practices make it possible to trust their repetition. The politics of the senses of a society attest that things happen routinely one way and not the other. But also, as already anticipated, trusting practices are based on the acceptance of the efficiency of the expert systems that manage the world as intermediaries between people and the external world. The experience of time is managed by clocks independently of monitoring by human beings.

Trust is a practice of feeling that operates at the level of expectations, it is a way of managing the threshold of reflective monitoring of action and the experience of sharing a perception horizon.

### 7.2.2 Characteristics of Digital Consumption as an "Epistemologem"

In the virtual/mobile/digital world, consumption becomes an "epistemologem"[1] since it provides the "crude schemes" through which ideological practices are elaborated in their cognitive contents. That is, they mark how to understand perception beyond the fluidity of the perceived material. They shift some embodied ways of knowing to other ways of knowing. The immediate enjoyment achieved in and through consumption becomes a criterion for the demarcation of reality.

Given the planetary expansion of normalized societies whose immediate enjoyment through consumption is anchored in mimesis and compensation, consumption has become a key feeling practice for social structuring.

One of the first characteristics of digital consumption is that it can be displayed in three different moments that may or may not be consecutive and that may or may not be interrelated. Buying, wearing out, and communicating, these moments are the bearers of a "new" epistemology given that they configure understanding and explaining the world and actions.

#### 7.2.2.1 Buying

Buying, acquiring, and obtaining are social practices that involve practices of feeling that refer to the connection between desire, need, and constitution of the person, since having is associated with being in terms of the social existence of the person, even more so in capitalist contexts. The digitization of the purchase must be understood in this framework. The first step of digital consumption is closely related to the processes of commercialization, marketing, procurement, and financing of consumption. In this sense, the production, commercialization, and distribution of the satisfying or consumer object are, in general, the starting point to becoming digital.

Companies work with data mining, social networks, and the virtual/mobile/digital world in general to design and offer the products that people prefer, fundamentally associated with the evocation of emotions and axes of the current politics of sensibilities. Knowing about the object, perceiving the object, and being aware of the characteristics of the object are already acts of consumption and therefore have to do with the object of consumption in its phase of enjoyment, in its phase of power, and wear. It is in this sense that the purchase acquires a sense of epistemologem.

#### 7.2.2.2 To wear out

Enjoyment is connected with consumption from a primary phenomenological association: to enjoy is to extract the fruit of the object and to consume is to spend it. There is a dialectic in the whole dialectic of enjoyment, consumption, and object of destruction.

Digital consumption revolves around three senses that are closely related to what we have called "looking by touching". First, the tactile connection with the digital device that one has, second, the visual connection that one has or may have of the consumer object, and third, the possibility to add sound/listen to the selection and wear.

Digital activity is a practice of the senses that compromises the impact, recursively, of Industry 4.0 that already supposes it. It is an activity that involves a) the extractive industries, such as mega open-pit mining, lithium exploitation, and rare earth, b) the productive webs built around the mobile/digital/virtual (devices, network accesses, etc.), and c) the global and normalizing connections of large Internet corporations such as Google, Amazon, WeChat, etc. Consuming in the digital age, among other features, increasingly involves the presence of cognitive-affective processes of whoever produces the object, who sells it, and who acquires/enjoys it.

#### *7.2.2.3 Communicate*

Digital consumption renews, deepens, and facilitates a central component of the consumption/enjoyment connection: we consume to show. The "make see" is part of consumption. If nobody finds it, it is not consumed, it is not enjoyed in the same way, and not all the juice is extracted from the fruit. Enjoying is a dramaturgical act that only acquires full meaning with an audience, with stages, with preparation, with backstage. The digital also provides all the means for this trait to be made real.

Selfies, photos of the landscape, of food, of "typical" objects, of expected corporalities, of imperative happiness, and obligatory joy as dissolutive containment must be elaborated on the acts of consumption.

It must be enjoyed, it must be as it should be, which implies that it must follow the impulse of what does good to the enjoyer, what makes him happy, and what makes him enviable. Without showing, without demonstrating, without making public that they are having a good time, there is no validity of enjoyment and therefore no "real" digital consumption.

The consumer becomes a "digital enjoyment seeker". Buy and wear showing, where showing is not a post-consumption or an after-enjoyment, it is a dialectic that comes from the mandate to have a good time as a life structurer in the 21st century that produces a lack of differentiation between work and leisure.

Buying, spending, and communicating are three moments of the same consuming process that constitutes the "identity" of the digital consumer.

There is a materiality of digital desire because the motive, the motivator, the stirrer, and the mobilizing energy that all desire implies here combines instantaneity, intensity, and the possibility of registration. Nothing is desired if it cannot be shown. Because desire itself is an energy of life dramatized for the other, in which I only desire what, in some way, I can make see what I have experienced, and that is why the centrality of the record: photos, videos, texts, and audios are the ways of my desire.

In the framework of what has been developed, it is possible to observe how trust and consumption are central elements of the modifications of the world of virtual/mobile/digital life and thus constitute two of the axes of the transformations operated in knowing, feeling-thinking, and in the "critique/justification" of accepted certainties.

## 7.3 Towards a Political Epistemology Based on Hope in Digital Contexts

Human knowledge and the modes of criticism/justification of it operate within the framework of a political dispute about what the world is, who owns the knowledge, how it is distributed, and how it is elaborated/transformed.

The existence of a political epistemology of the social sciences has been the subject of discussion in the social and human sciences since its inception, embodied in various polemics and disputes such as naturalism and romanticism, explanation and understanding, among others.

In this context, and in tension with trust and digital consumption, it is interesting to ask ourselves about hope as the basis of a political epistemology in order to end this chapter and this book on how to study emotions in the context of the world of virtual/mobile/digital life.

Hope is an emotion connected with the development of the social sciences since its inception, thematized either as utopia, revolution, and/or optimism. The "claim" of human beings regarding the future, what can be modified, and what is pertinent to expect was and is a central topic of knowing.

It is possible to synthesize in the following way the traits that transform hope into a practice of feeling that impacts the elaboration of a political epistemology that dialectically creates tensions to trust and consumption.

The first trait is that hope is anticipatory practice of the future, people have no hope but it is not connected with an action that is going to be sent to the future for its realization. The question for tomorrow is a "cartography" of the present. One of the edges of the social practices that are modified in the virtual/mobile/digital world is the capacity and management of time and the deployment of human action in the unanchored/disconnected from the time/space packages.

One of the important things about the future is that human beings do it in the present without "discontinuity" of a here/now; it is in this sense that hope is not associated with chronology, hope is associated with the dialectic of time and space, how we inhabit the past; because it is our present, the future is not simply made from now on, it is made.

A second feature is that hope is a being that inhabits the future. Human beings have the possibility of developing a practice that is inhabiting, presenting the past, and instantiating what is expected and what is projected. Hope is a proxy indicator of the ability to foresee, to see in advance, since it is an experience, it is not a "mere idea". In this direction, hope means that the construction of the indicated habitability implies at least three things: a) hope is a being that gives shelter, b) hope is a being that puts the other in a place of proximity, and c) hope is a being that inhabits the future because it is a point of reference in our advance towards the future. It is a radical critique of the usual predation of the world "using a functional plexus of variables" which operates as a scientifically consecrated social horizon of prediction.

A third trait of hope is perceptible from a germinal analogy of the explanation: hope is always a fruit. Hope is planting something for tomorrow, it is taking up the idea of the etymology of happiness associated with agriculture, it is taking up the idea of the root, that being means a plant that is planted to be planted. Work, wait, obtain, and distribute are all practices that have been digitally transformed in this century and that influence how to explain the production and reproduction of the world. "Ex-plain" is precisely to unroll what is to grow.

So this agrarian metaphor of hope takes us to a third feature in terms of the surface of understanding of the world made between knowledge, wisdom, and beliefs. Having hope is the power of a reconstruction of being with the logic of the fruit.

Being for the fruit involves epistemic criteria that go beyond the efficacy and efficiency of the instrumental, associating knowing with a geo-culture of wisdom.

In close connection with the above, and as the fourth epistemic feature of hope, it can be noted that through it we have the certainty of an anticipated knowledge, of knowing that something one produces is going to have certain consequences where said consequences are not only linked to a logic of "instrumental rationality". In this way, the goals are not at the end, but it is by working on the goals that guarantees the results. There are always other goals that guarantee other results: knowledge is an impossible quest to "catch/fossilize".

The fifth feature of hope as an epistemic resource is the radical politics that, as an anticipatory practice of the future, is complex, indeterminate, relational, and reciprocal. It is founded on a radical intersubjectivity, a radical constructivity, a recognition of the material conditions of existence that leaves out any form of miserabilism, romanticism, and enlightenment and is founded on a gaze that is intersectional, post-speciesist, and post-colonial.

A political epistemology the virtual/mobile/digital world finds in hope traces of modification of the validity criteria, the forms of explanation, the logic of prediction, and the goals of the social sciences.

## Note

1 The term is thought of in the cross between "mythologeme", as a narrative that founds a practice of knowledge, and what Andrew Collier (1989) elaborated as an "epistemoid", in terms of an ontology and style of thinking that derive from science but without being it.

## Reference list

Baquero Rodríguez, M. J., Aldana Gutiérrez, Y., & Rivero Ortiz, G. A. (2014). The construction of facebook as an affective prosthesis. *Íkala, Revista de lenguaje y cultura, 19*(2),149–166.

Barbalet, J. (2014). The structure of Guanxi: Resolving problems of network assurance. *Theory and Society, 43*(1), 51–69. https://doi.org/10.1007/s11186-013-9211-2

Basabe de Quintale, M. C., & Durán Rodríguez, E. (2013). Salud mental y expresión de las emociones en el facebook. *Anuario Electrónico de Estudios en Comunicación Social "Disertaciones", 6*(2), 88–111.

Brun, G., & Kuenzle, D. (2018). A new role for emotions in epistemology?. In Brun, G., Dogluoglu, U., & Kuenzle, D. (eds.), *Epistemology and Emotions* (pp. 1–31). Ashgate Publishing Company.

Collier, A. (1989). *Scientific Realism and Socialist Thougth.* Harvester Wheatsheaf.

De Sena, A., & Scribano, A. (2020). *Social Policies and Emotions. A Look from the Global South.* Palgrave Macmillan.

De Vasconcelos Gico, V., & Hecker Luz, L. (2017). As redes sociais digitais e a humanização do parto no contexto das Epistemologias do Sul. *Revista FAMECOS: mídia, cultura e tecnologia, 24*(1). https://doi.org/10.15448/1980-3729.2017.1.24801

García Gutiérrez, A. (2011). Desclassification in knowledge organization: A post-epistemological essay. *Transinformação, 23*(1), 5–14.

Grützmann, A., Felício Macedo, F. M., & Zambalde, A. L. (2013). Knowledge management and innovation: The role of virtual social networks in innovative consumer behavior. *Journal of Technology Management & Innovation, 8*(1), 209–220.

Marteleto, R. M. (2015). Epistemologia social e cultura digital: reflexões em torno das formas de escritas na web. *Em Questão, 21*(3), 9–25.

Mitchell, J. (2017). The epistemology of emotional experience. *Dialectica, 71,* 57–84. https://doi.org/10.1111/1746-8361.12171.

Müller, J. M. (2017). How (not) to think of emotions as evaluative attitudes. *Dialectica, 71,* 281–308. https://doi.org/10.1111/1746-8361.12192.

Russell Hochschild, A. (2019). Emotions and society. *Emotions and Society, 1*(1), 9–13. https://doi.org/10.1332/263168919X15580836411805.

Scribano, A. (2016). *Investigación social basada en la creatividad/expresividad.* Estudios Sociológicos Editora.

Scribano, A. (2017). *Normalization, Enjoyment and Bodies/emotions: Argentine Sensibilities.* Nova Science Publishers.

Scribano, A. (2021). *Colonization of Inner Planet. 21st Century Social Theory from the Politics of Sensibilities.* Routledge.

Scribano, A., & Korstanje, M. E. (2017). Emotions and epistemology: a path for reconsideration in the 21st century. *International Journal of Human Rights and Constitutional Studies, 5*(2), 111–129.

Scribano, A., & Lisdero, P. (Eds.). (2019). *Digital Labour, Society and Politics of Sensibilities.* Palgrave Macmillan.

Sztompka, P. (1999). *Trust: A Sociological Theory.* Cambridge University Press.

Thomson-Jones, K., & Moser, S. (2019). The philosophy of digital art. In Zalta, E. N., (ed.), *The Stanford Encyclopedia of Philosophy* (Spring 2021 ed.). Retrieved from https://plato.stanford.edu/archives/spr2021/entries/digital-art/.

Vanello, D. (2020). Affect, motivational states, and evaluative concepts. *Synthese, 197,* 4617–4636. https://doi.org/10.1007/s11229-019-02120-0

# INDEX

Page numbers in **bold** denote tables, in *italic* denote figures

Ingram Content Group UK Ltd.
Milton Keynes UK
UKHW020426100323
418353UK00015B/108